Learn Indonesian by Association

Indoglyphs ™

The easy playful way to learn a new language.

Written by: Jai Nanda

Published in the UK by BadGoose Publishing 2014

Jai Nanda asserts the moral right to be identified as the Author of this work.

Indoglyhps & Wordglyphs are a trademarks for the Authors Indonesian & other language learning products.

Copyright © Jai Nanda

ISBN-13: ISBN-978-1494960056

Learn Indonesian by Association -
Indoglyps
First Edition

All rights reserved. No part of this book may be reproduced or transmitted in any form or by any means, electronic or mechanical, including photocopying, recording, or by any information storage and retrieval system without the written permission of the author, except where permitted by law.

Dedicated to:

Mira Maniez who inspired me to learn Indonesian and remains my muse.

Jelila for your example and passion. Without you I never would have started.

Olive Harvey for always being there.

Contents

Indoglyphs™ Language Learning. 1
Why it works 3
    Research Evidence.. 5
    Using this book... 6
    How to learn a new word. 8
    Your First Words in Indonesian 10
    Notations used 11
    Avoiding confusions 12
    Handling Grammar. 13
A little bit about Indonesia 14
    Overview 14
    Customs 15
Let's get stuck in 17
    Every day vocabulary 17
    How to check you've integrated the words. 19
    Here are a few more words... 21
    Using the words you've learned so far 24
I , My ,Me - You, Your 25
Let's learn some more words 27
    Be my guest at the Airport tomorrow 27
    The Cat's in the toilet at the restaurant. 31
Past, present, future 35
Soak up some more vocab 37
    Wake up thirsty without clothes 37
    Hot week to move out the village 40
Some sentence structure 44
    Descriptive word order 44
    Making Plurals 45

Practice using the words you've learned 46
Get some more vocab 47
    Now you're nearly fluent! 47
    Don't cook ice cream on your Birthday 51
Greetings - Times of the Day 54
    Good morning, afternoon, evening & good night 54
Phrases & Slang out and about 57
    How's it going and others! 57
    No Problem 58
    Colloquial city and sms 59
Sentence practice part 1 62
Some more great words to learn 63
    Late for the dance party 63
    White sand, weather and sauce 67
More words for your Indonesian journey 70
    Sorry for the rain and mosquitoes 70
Yes you can learn many words 73
    Rubbish Taxi's and a place to sleep 73
    Get ready to start the download 77
Sentence practice part 2 80
Unusual Foods and fruits 81
Never, ever, possessions and first. 84
    How to use ever and never. 84
    How to indicate possessions & "the" - Nya 85
    How to say I'm doing that first - Dulu 86
You can remember so many more... 87
    Sit down, have a Coffee 87
    Old pancakes and black phones 90
Chat ups, romance and lovers! 93
    Darling, I love your eyes 93

Sentence practice part 3 97
Words on the home straight 98
   Is it true your Father smells? 98
   Small change for your family under the tree 102
Numbers & Money 105
   Learning your numbers and all about money. 105
   One to Ten (1- 10) 106
   Eleven to Nineteen (11 - 19) 108
   The tens (20, 30, 40….) 109
   Hundreds, Thousands and Millions 110
   Ordinals 112
Date and Time 114
   Months and Days of the week 114
   Month names 114
   What's the date? 116
   Days of the week 117
   Seasons 119
   Telling the time 120
Sentence practise part 4 121
Congratulations 122
About the Author 123
   Personal note from the Author 124
   Connect with Jai 125
Answers to sections & quizzes 126
   Past, Present, Future practice 126
   Numbers check 127
   Sentence practice 1 128
   Sentence practice 2 129
   Sentence practice 3 130
   Sentence practice 4 131

Pronunciation **132**
    Vowels 132
    Consonants: 133
    Alphabet 135
Index **1**
Your Notes. **6**

Indoglyphs™ Language Learning.

Learn Indonesian fast with this amazing memory technique. It's easy, engaging and long-lasting, no more book worming with boring lists of words - **Indoglyphs™** sets you free to learn in your way, at your pace and with great results. We already know a language so why not use it to add new words onto what you already know. Using this method, you can learn hundreds of words remarkably quickly.

Indoglyphs™ works by creating associations from the English words we already know, to the new words we want to learn. The more outrageous or funny the association, the easier it is to remember. The more vivid the experience, the more you remember about it!

Get Wise!

Hi – my name's James.

As an instructor in Laughter Yoga, Improvised Comedy and Dance, I love using humour and word play to learn and have fun. This book is how I rapidly learned Indonesian whilst in Bali. I started with a course going through a workbook twice a week for a month. It was so dry and such a struggle to learn the words, I thought "I'll never manage this!" Then I remembered a technique I'd come across and started to use it and adapt it to learn Indonesian.

It's a memory technique (I call a teachnique) that I've augmented with my own methods to make it more effective. It totally turned around my belief that I couldn't learn a new language – what I found was – I just didn't know how to have fun doing so! That's what I want to share with you, fun effective learning.

Indoglyphs™ Language Learning
www.wordglyphs.com

Page | 2

No more learning by rote, boring repetition and frustration. This book provides you with a remarkably easy way to learn hundreds of Indonesian words quickly and playfully. So dive in, enjoy yourself and add to your vocabulary faster than you ever imagined possible!

Indoglyphs™ Language Learning
www.wordglyphs.com

Page | 3

Why it works

Our method of learning is 3 times more effective than traditional learning. It uses a consequence about how our brains work, (that is little known), to record new words in our memory, quickly and effectively.

"I expect you all to be independent, innovative, critical thinkers who will do exactly as I say!"

The left side of our brain is primarily involved with logic and language (unless you are left handed). This side on its own can learn new words, but it's a little bit like trying to glue new words onto a piece of paper on a windy day - not many stick!

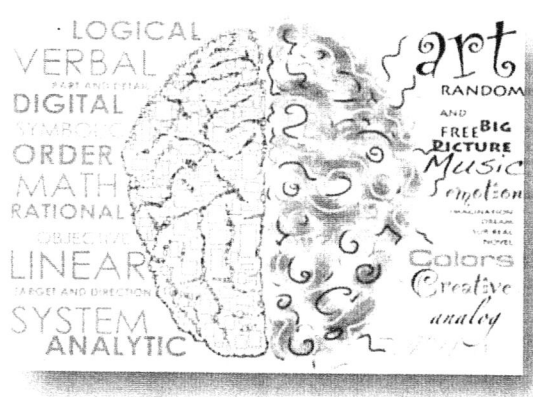

The right side of the brain is involved in emotions, creativity and intuition. This side can imagine, invent and visualise which is great for learning new experiences, but doesn't do language. So guess what...

When we bring these two parts together, magic happens. By getting emotionally involved and imagining or visualising *(more on how to do that later)*, we create strong experiences which

Indoglyphs™ Language Learning
www.wordglyphs.com

stimulate learning. When we use this with another brain trick, called hooking, we remember words very easily.

Hooking is where we already have an idea or thing remembered and we hook (or link on) something else on to it. For example, If you already have a basis in using a computer, it's easier to learn how to use a smart phone. It's the same with art or any skill. Here we simply use the English words we now to hook on new Indonesian words and it's highly effective.

Indoglyphs™ Language Learning
www.wordglyphs.com

Research Evidence

Studies have been carried out by Atkinson & Raugh showing a marked improvement in retention of language using a word association or a mnemonic method of learning.

The experiments compared learning using, what they called, a keyword method of learning, versus a control group, who used traditional methods of learning such as repetition and by rote.

Participants were given an English keyword that sounds like the foreign word they were learning, and then a mental image of that keyword, essentially an association. The results when learning Spanish were remarkable.

- **88% of the words were retained using the method**
- **28% of the words retained learning by rote**

For learning Spanish - the results were **over 3 times better** than learning using traditional methods.

The same research team also found that retention significantly improved. They found people achieved:

- **50% Better immediate recall**
- **75% Improvement longer term**

And this was learning Russian, which is far more difficult to associate than Indonesian.

"I found this research subsequent to learning Indonesian with Indoglyphs. Personally, my retention and long term recall has been remarkable, but of course, I can't prove it to you. The best thing is to try it for yourself" - James.

Let's see how to use this book to support you most effectively...

Indoglyphs™ Language Learning
www.wordglyphs.com

Using this book

This book is about learning Indonesian vocabulary and simple grammar so you can speak and write in Indonesian. It presents lists of simple everyday words along with associations and visualisations which activate your memory for learning. You read the association for a word, close your eyes and visualise or experience the scene or situation in your own way. An incredible number of words can be learnt quickly and permanently in a short time using this simple method.

If you find visualising difficult (actually seeing something in your mind's eye), then simply try and get the feeling of the sentence, hear the words in your head as if you are experiencing, sensing or hearing it happen in front of you, or imagine yourself acting it out.

Free your Mind...

Each of us has a primary method of learning - Visual (pictures - images), Auditory (listening - words) and Kinaesthetic (more physical - solid). Most people are Visual these days due to the influences of media, Television etc. I've found the best thing to do is to "Play" with each way and see what works best for YOU, you might be surprised! The more you practice, the easier and quicker it gets. You become more proficient the more you learn - how many other language techniques make you more effective the more you learn!

Now you can relax - I have done all the hard work for you and made the associations so you don't have to. Let your imagination fly - the more richly you can experience the association, the stronger the memory of the words you will have.

Indoglyphs™ Language Learning
www.wordglyphs.com

The associations may not present an exact pronunciation of the word you are learning. Often there is no exact match to hook the new word to and so an approximation is required. This is not as important as you might think. The association will give you the ability to retrieve the word you want from your memory, like a key to a lock, it opens the door. Your mind then presents you with the actual word you want.

The approximation to the actual word will gives you the basis to easily retrieve your new word from memory. I have given pronunciation tips where it's not obvious and you can use the pronunciation section to get it exactly right.

You'll find the pronunciation section at the back of the book, but for now, the most important thing is to **roll your R's**, pronounce **C** is **Ch** as in **Chair** and to swallow your **G's** like the first **G in Gang**. Most other letters are pronounced very close to English, which is a great help for us.

Let's look at an example of how to learn a word...

Indoglyphs™ Language Learning
www.wordglyphs.com

How to learn a new word.

Here's an example of how to learn the word **Good** in Indonesian.

The word for **Good** is **Bagus**.

For each word being learned, the English word, then the Indonesian word is presented. In this case:

Good - Bagus

Next is a sentence for you to make the association between the two, by using words you already know as a hook, for the new word you want to learn.

Read the sentence then imagine the scene (visualising, hearing, experiencing as you wish). The more vivid and the stronger your experience, the more effective your learning will be.

Try this example below for the word Good.

Good - Bagus

Imagine a <u>bad goose</u> that mended its ways and is now going around doing <u>good</u> deeds like washing up.

The words underlined are the ones we are associating.

Take your time with the scene. Imagine it happening, seeing it in your mind's eye, hearing the sounds or words, feeling the sensations... The more colour, texture, and sounds you add the more it will lodge in your memory.

Indoglyphs™ Language Learning
www.wordglyphs.com

This example works very well as it is fairly ridiculous because Geese never do good deeds and especially washing up! (*At least not the ones that chased me the last time I met them*).

Remember, the more outlandish the idea, the stronger the memory that is created.

Once you've used your imagination to picture, feel or sense the scene, think of the word <u>Good</u> and rehearse the scene in your mind one more time.

That's it! It's now in your memory.

When you want to say a word in Indonesian like **Good**, you will immediately have the picture of a Goose in your mind, or the sensation of it, or the word, and then you'll remember the Goose was a **bad goose** and then you'll have the word for Good in Indonesian right there - **bagus**.

The words I have chosen for associations in the book also give you the pronunciation. So the **ba** of **bad** and the **goos** of **goose** are exactly how to say the word. In some cases, where it's unclear, I have given guidance to help with the pronunciation.

After a while, the association disappears *(if you're worried about having errant Geese running around your head)* and you just 'know' the word you need.

Using this method you can learn hundreds of words in a very short space of time. That's all there is to it. It is amazing how effective it is. Recruiting both sides of your brain to learn new words really works!

Let's learn a few words right now...

Indoglyphs™ Language Learning
www.wordglyphs.com

Your First Words in Indonesian

Hello/Hi - Halo/Hai
It's the same so imagine saying hello to a person wrapped in an Indonesian flag.

When words are the same or very similar we use the Indonesian flag as the association so we remember it's the same in both Languages. (The flag is red and white).

Yes - Ya
Imagine you go to a posh event and everyone there has double chins and says "yar" instead of yes.

Please - Tolong
Imagine when you break down you ask "please I'd need a tow along the road to get me home".

The next few pages cover notations used, how not grouping words by category aids learning, how we cover grammar in the book and a little bit about Indonesia.

You can skip these if you like and start right now by jumping to the chapter **Lets get stuck in**.

Indoglyphs™ Language Learning
www.wordglyphs.com

Notations used

The book uses some short hand notations to help with pronunciation and explanations. The following are used throughout the book:

(Pr: xxxxxx)

When you see (Pr: xxxxxx) this means that the xxxxxx is a word to help you with the pronunciation of the word you are learning.

(Lit: xxxxx xxxx)

When you see (Lit: xxxxx xxxx) this means that the xxxx xxxx is a literal translation of the sentence or word before it.

The literal translation will help to make the sentence structure obvious for you, as the word order or the way words are used, are not always the same is in English.

Indoglyphs™ Language Learning
www.wordglyphs.com

Avoiding confusions

When learning new words, there is a temptation to learn associated words at the same time, e.g. Good Morning, Afternoon, Evening and Good Night, colours, directions and so on. Also, it's the same with opposites, hot and cold, good and bad...

When we learn related words at the same time, our brain finds it harder to remember which of the choices is the one we need. This is also true for any Indonesian words we are learning that look or sound similar.

For this reason, I have done my best to keep similar related words and Indonesian words that look or sound similar separate. This makes it much easier to retain and re-produce the right word for the given situation. That's why the book is not divided up into, **Greetings**, **At the Restaurant** and so on like other language learning and phrase books. It just doesn't work very well for us to learn related words at the same time. it is a useful structure for a phrase book, however this book is primarily about learning vocabulary so you don't need one.

Not all words lend themselves to be learnt separately, such as numbers and dates, so I've given those in their own sections. On the whole, learning associated words separately is far more effective.

With opposites, you can give yourself a leg up by learning one side of the opposite and then the word for not. This way you can double the number of expressions you have, avoiding the need to learn a words opposite!

Handling Grammar.

Having an extensive vocabulary to draw on in a language is an amazing help, but, there are some rules to languages that put the words in the right order and certain modifiers that change some verbs!

Fortunately, in Indonesian, there are very few modifiers for tenses, e.g. what happened in the past, what's happening now or what's going to happen in the future. In general, for spoken Indonesian, verb modifiers are mostly dropped! This is great news for us!

Some of the word order is not the same as in English, so I have added sections in the book to help you out. This will help you get the word order more correct. The aim of this book, as in any communication, is to be understood, and most of the time, even if the word order is mixed up, you'll get the message across. If not, Indonesians are amazing helpful at correcting you.

I have interspersed the sections for tenses, word order and other items (such as colloquialisms) throughout the book as a learning aid and to keep you stimulated. Indonesian is a much more simple language than English, but we still need to know how to understand and map that simplicity!

The next section is a little background about Indonesia – but if you want to dive straight into learning words – go ahead and skip it!

Indoglyphs™ Language Learning
www.wordglyphs.com

A little bit about Indonesia

Overview

Indonesian is spoken by over 200 million people in Indonesia and can also be used (with a few word exceptions) in Malaysia (28 million) where it originated. Indonesia (*derived from the Greek words Indós and nèsos, meaning "island"*) is made up of 922 inhabited Islands with more than 300 native languages between them.

Indonesian was established as the official language of Indonesia in 1945 and is the common language for all the Indonesian Islands. That being said, it is only the mother tongue of a few of the major cities, predominantly Jakarta. As the official language it's the language used on sign posts, for sms notifications, legal documents, at the airport, in fact anywhere where official information is written down. If you are travelling in Indonesia, it's the best language to learn as you'll be able to communicate with the most number of people and find your way around.

Besides language, there are some cultural considerations that you might find useful to take into account when communicating. Communication isn't just about the words, it's about understanding and relating to the person you are talking to.

Several of the Indonesian customs may seem strange to you, but to avoid causing offence it is good to know a few things about the background of Indonesia and some do's and don'ts.

Indoglyphs™ Language Learning
www.wordglyphs.com

Customs

The primary religion of Indonesia is Muslim. Most religions are represented across Indonesia, Christian, Buddhist and Hindu amongst them with Bali being the only Island which is predominately Hindu.

When meeting someone for the first time you can shake hands, however, with women, wait to see if their hand is offered first.

Be aware that, because Indonesians are used to living in close families and in overcrowded situations, their idea of personal space may not be the same as yours. Often you might feel like you are having your space invaded, but it's perfectly natural for them. Bear this in mind so you can avoid getting upset or annoyed!

A man does not display affection for a woman in public. Although it does not seem to be frowned on for Westerners to do it, you may cause offence if you publically display affection for an Indonesian of the opposite sex. This is not such an issue in the big cities, more in rural areas or places like Bali.

The head is considered to be where the spirit resides for Indonesians (and most Asians). Simply avoid touching others heads, no matter how cute the kid looks.

Most people are not punctual – relax – you're in Indonesia!

These are a few pointers to help you on your way. Generally, I have found the Indonesians to be pretty tolerant, but I also like to promote respect for their customs, and hope you do too.

Indoglyphs™ Language Learning
www.wordglyphs.com

This map of Indonesia show how diverse the people are.

Distribution of Indonesian Religions.

Let's get stuck in

Every day vocabulary

Here are some words that will allow you to have some basic conversation extremely quickly. Later in the section you can check your learning and see some examples of how to use the words you have learnt.

Above all - HAVE FUN!!!

 *Remember - the more vivid you make the association, the stronger the memory of each word will be.*

How are you - Apa Kabar
Imagine a magician asking <u>how are you</u> and waving his wand with an <u>abra kadabra</u>.

I - Saya
Imagine you meet a man who sighs a lot and he introduced himself, it is <u>I</u> the <u>Sigher</u>!

Name - Nama
Imagine trying to <u>Name A</u> famous person!

Goodbye - Sampai Jumpa
Imagine saying <u>goodbye</u> to a pie made of sand and your old Jumper! <u>Goodbye Sandpie, Jumper.</u>

To - Ke (Pr: ke as in kerb)
Imagine going <u>to</u> your car and you get interrupted and only get as far as saying the <u>C</u> of the word <u>car</u>!

Indoglyphs™ Language Learning
www.wordglyphs.com

No/Not -Tidak
Imagine you are bird watching and your friend asks you "Is that the rare tea drinking duck?", you reply "No, it's not the Tea Duck, it's a Bali duck!".

Understand - Mengerti
Imagine some mung beans getting your tea. You can't understand how mung beans can get our tea! Mung-ge(t)-tea.

Price - Harga(nya)
Imagine you are buying something and you must bargain harder for a good price, you can't get it so you say 'nya' I don't want it!

Go - Pergi
Imagine you have a cat called Gi and wherever you go makes it Purr! Purr Gi.

Language - Bahasa
Imagine a Sheep that can't Baa, has a definite Language problem.

How to check you've integrated the words.

This section helps you to find out which words you've remembered and which you need to review. This is a really important part of the book because the more you recall the words, the stronger your memory of them will be.

From the list below, first cover the English column and say the word you have just learned in Indonesian out loud. Then cover the Indonesian column and say the corresponding English word out loud. This helps you to translate in both directions. If you only translate one way, you may find that you can speak Indonesian, but not understand it!

The words in the practise list are intentionally not in the original order. We tend to remember things at the beginning and end of lists, so mixing up the order will help you remember more effectively.

Any words that you don't remember go back over the association and then do the check again. Remember to congratulate yourself on what you have achieved and avoid putting yourself down for what you didn't remember. Positive reinforcement works!

 *If you are interested in writing in Indonesian - write the words down as well as saying them to check you have the spelling accurate.*

Here's your first practice list to check the words you've learned so far...

Indoglyphs™ Language Learning
www.wordglyphs.com

Checking what you've learned

English	Indonesian
Name	Nama
Goodbye	Sampai Jumpa
No/Not	Tidak
Language	Bahasa
To	Ke
How are you	Apa Kabar
Understand	Mengerti
Price	Harga(nya)
Go	Pergi
I (my)	Saya

Remember – go back over any that you haven't remembered yet!

Revisiting the practice by recalling helps cement the words in your memory.

Indoglyphs™ Language Learning
www.wordglyphs.com

Here are a few more words...

Where - Di Mana (where something is)
Imagine looking on a map to find <u>where</u> a huge manor house built in the shape of the letter D. <u>Where</u> is that <u>D manor</u>?

OK, Fine - Baik (most used in response to 'how are you'?)

Imagine it's <u>OK</u> to ride your new <u>bike</u> with a frame made from the letters, <u>OK</u>.

Want - Mau
Imagine a child that says M instead of N saying, it's mine and I <u>want</u> it <u>mow</u>.

Book - Buku
Imagine you are surprised to find your <u>book</u>, there's my <u>book Ooo</u>.

You - Anda
Imagine an Italian meeting <u>you</u> for the first time, they say, <u>and A</u> - you are?

Finish(ed) - Selesai (doing something)
Imagine being a salesman who knows you are <u>finished</u> learning about sales when you can <u>sell A Sigh</u>.

Thank you - Terima kasih
Imagine you tear the seat of your taxi's car as you get out and he says "<u>Thank you</u> for <u>tearing my car seat</u>"

Who - Siapa
Imagine thinking, I wonder <u>who</u> that is with the pipe and slippers. You <u>see a Pa</u>, that's who.

Indoglyphs™ Language Learning
www.wordglyphs.com

How much/ How many - Berapa
Imagine at the market you want to know <u>how much</u> for the socks but you can't hear because of the rapping bears. <u>How many</u> <u>bear-rappers</u> are there?

Stay (live) - Tinggal
Imagine you feel a <u>tingle</u> when you <u>stay</u> in indonesia.

That - Itu
Imagine you are shopping so insistently that you'll have <u>that</u> hat and take <u>it too</u>!

Can - Bisa
Imagine it's your Birthday and there's no way you <u>can</u> <u>be sad</u> with so many people coming to your party.

Checking what you've learned

English	Indonesian
Thank You	Terima kasih
That	Itu
Finished	Selesai
Can	Bisa
Who	Siapa
How much/many	Berapa
You (Your)	Anda/Kamu
OK	Fine Baik
Where (is)	Di Mana
Book	Buku
Want	Mau
Stay	Tinggal

Congratulate yourself for what you remembered and go back over any that haven't or leave them until later!

Go easy on yourself, the more you appreciate your accomplishments (rather than berate your failures), the happier you are to learn more.

Indoglyphs™ Language Learning
www.wordglyphs.com

Using the words you've learned so far

Now you've got a range of things you can say with just these few words. Amazing how quickly we can communicate!

Here are some examples of using the words so far in sentences. I've added the literal translation of the words so you can get an idea of some word order (which we will cover later) and for a flavour of the language usage.

Phrase	Translation	Literally
Hello, how are you?	Hai, apa kabar?	Hi, what news?
Fine, thanks!	Baik, terima makasih!	OK/fine thank you
What's your name?	Siapa nama anda?	Who name you?
My name's John	Saya nama John	I name John
I would like that	Saya mau itu	I want that
How much is that?	Berapa harganya?	How many (price) is that?
I don't understand	Saya tidak mengerti	I no/not understand
Where do you live?	Di mana Anda tinggal?	Where you stay/live?
Are you finished?	Anda selesai?	You finished?
I want to go to...	Saya mau pergi ke...	I want go to...

Even with these few words at your disposal you can greet people, ask their name and give them yours, ask how much something is, ask to go somewhere and say if you understand or not - just in a few minutes.

Indoglyphs™ Language Learning
www.wordglyphs.com

I, My, Me - You, Your

Indonesian is far simpler than English. When you want to talk about yourself, **(I, me)**, or refer to anything you posses **(my)** or someone else and what they posses **(you, your)** it's greatly simplified. There are only two words to consider and where they are used in a sentence gives their meaning.

Here's a handy table to explain.

English	Indonesian	Use
I	Saya	Before
My	Saya	After
Me	Saya	After
You	Anda	Before & After
Your	Anda	After

Let's look at this in practice...

Use of Saya

Generally at the beginning of a sentence **Saya** means I and at the end it's **my or me**.

"I want that" is "Saya mau itu" (lit: I want that)

"My Book" is "Buku Saya" (lit: Book I)

Indoglyphs™ Language Learning
www.wordglyphs.com

"Please understand me" is "Tolong mengerti saya"

Use of Anda

Generally at the beginning of a sentence **Anda** means you and at the end it's **your**.

"Do you want that" is "Anda mau itu"

"Your Book" is "Buku anda" (lit: book you)

"Where are you?" is "Di mana anda?" (lit: Where you?)

In the last two cases, **Anda** goes in the same place in the sentence as English!

Formal/Informal

Saya and **Anda** also have informal forms **Aku** and **Kamu**.

You will be fine with the formal form of the words, but you may hear **Kamu** used a lot particularly with the younger generation. **Aku** is generally reserved for sweethearts, and is considered a bit cheesy by the younger set!

You - Kamu
Imagine a young you is great at animal impressions and can moo.

I - Aku
Imagine when I call my lover - I coo.

Indoglyphs™ Language Learning
www.wordglyphs.com

Let's learn some more words

Be my guest at the Airport tomorrow

Rice - Nasi
Imagine you take your friend to see how rice grows, they think it grows on trees, and you show them a plant and say 'na see, rice grows from the ground'.

Will - Akan
Imagine you are at an airfield and you will learn to fly, then you can tell everyone "I can".

Learn(ing) / Study - Belajar
Imagine you are learning chemistry and you need to use a huge bell jar to contain all your notes.

Be my guest, Go ahead or Please - Silahkan
(When you are offering something)
Imagine you offer a can of drink to your friend and say, go ahead, be my guest try open this silly can.

Airport - Bandara
Imagine you get stopped by security for wearing a Bandana into the Airport!

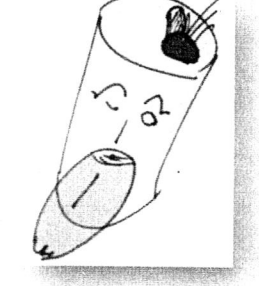

House - Rumah
Imagine an Italian comes round your house and remarks – ah, nice Rooma' in your house!

Just - Saja
Imagine you just arrived after a party and the house is such a mess.

Very - Sekali (Formal)
Imagine you are a Knight called Lee and you very much want a car suitable for a Sir with your name on it, Sir Car Lee.

Indoglyphs™ Language Learning
www.wordglyphs.com

Beach - Pantai.
Imagine you go to the <u>beach</u> and everyone has a pan around their necks. You ask someone and they explain it's the new fashion beach wear called a <u>Pan Tie</u>.

Water - Air (Pr: Eyer)
Imagine you now drop your H's as you lift some <u>water</u> '<u>igher</u> and 'igher.

Know - Tahu (Pr: Tow as in Towel)
Imagine a friend denies taking your Towel from the bathroom –, but you <u>know</u> that '<u>towel</u>' is yours.

Tomorrow - Besok
Imagine <u>tomorrow</u> you go to the cleaners to wash your best socks but you only take one <u>best sock</u> at a time!

There is/are - Ada (like have)
Imagine <u>there is</u> an <u>Adder</u> in the grass in your garden, you turn around and suddenly <u>there are</u> Adders everywhere!

Problem - Masala
Imagine you are in an Indian restaurant – call the waiter over and tell them there's a <u>problem</u> with your chicken '<u>Masala</u>'.

Swimming - Renang
Imagine you want to go for a <u>swim</u> but they <u>rename</u> your favourite <u>swimming</u> pool so you can't find it.

Already - Sudah
Imagine you friend telling you all about Sue and her bad habit of picking her nose. You say, "But I <u>already</u> met <u>Sue, da</u>!"

Indoglyphs™ Language Learning
www.wordglyphs.com

Brown – Coklat
Imagine you trod in something <u>brown</u> and your relief when you realise that you just trod in bar of <u>chocolate</u>.

Where – Ke mana (to go)
Imagine <u>where</u> you desperately want to go is the new apple <u>core manor</u>.

Checking what you've learned

English	Indonesian
Just	Saja
Will	Akan
Be my guest/If you please	Silahkan
Swimming	Renang
Very	Sekali
Airport	Bandara
Rice	Nasi
Brown	Coklat
Tomorrow	Besok
House	Rumah
Problem	Masala
Learn(ing)	Belajar
Already	Sudah
Beach	Pantai
Where (to go)	Ke mana
How long	Berapa lama
Know	Tahu
Water	Air
There is/are	Ada

Remember you can go back over any that haven't quiet stuck!

Indoglyphs™ Language Learning
www.wordglyphs.com

The Cat's in the toilet at the restaurant.

Coconut - Kelapa
Imagine a dog drinking keys from a coconut shell. That dogs a key lapper.

Sugar - Gula
Imagine your French friend telling you he spilt some sugar, now there is Goo la (Goo there).

Cat - Kucing (Pr: c as ch in chair)
Imagine a Cat stuck in a till. You open the till and it makes the sound, ke-ching!

There - Di sana
Imagine you are camping and need to go the toilet block all the way over there to De-Sanatise the toilet.

Toilet - Toilet
Imagine a toilet with an Indonesian flag in it!

Later - Nanti
Imagine you are excited that later you will go to your Nan's for Tea and have Nan-Tea.

Restaurant - Warung/Restoran
Imagine you enter a hostile Restaurant where there is a war run from the kitchen about the missing "T".

Indoglyphs™ Language Learning
www.wordglyphs.com

Big - Besar
Imagine you get really lost in a really <u>big</u> Turkish <u>bazaar</u>.

When - Kapan
Imagine you are wondering when your new car frying pan accessory is going to arrive. <u>When</u> is that <u>car pan</u> going to be delivered?

Tea - Teh
Imagine a <u>tea</u> cup with the handle shaped like the letter 'a'. Now break off the handle and you have a cup of <u>Te</u>.

Red - Merah
Imagine you are <u>red</u> from sun burn at a horse trial where there are so many horses you can see a <u>mare a</u> minute.

Drink - Minum
Imagine you are in a coffee shop and you order the <u>minimum</u> size <u>drink</u>.

Excuse me - Permisi
Imagine a sign on the grass in Italy that says, <u>Excuse me</u>, no <u>permissi</u>-on to walk on the grass.

Yesterday - Kemarin
Imagine <u>yesterday</u>, you caught a Marlin fish in the shape of a K. Newspaper headlines report man catches <u>K - Marlin</u>.

Eat - Makan
Imagine you <u>make an</u> omelette to <u>eat</u> which is the most delicious thing you ever ate.

Motor Bike - Sepeda motor
Imagine that you are out on your <u>Motor Bike</u> and another <u>speedy motor</u> zips past you.

Without - Tanpa
Imagine that <u>without</u> sun cream you will get your Father brown, now you can <u>Tan pa</u>.

Beli - Buy
Imagine you go to an amazing store to <u>buy</u> some shoes and you cannot <u>beli</u>eve how cheap they are.

Now - Sekarang
Imagine you telephone someone they ask you what you are doing <u>now</u>, and you say, this <u>sec' I rang</u>?

Checking what you've learned

English	Indonesian
Sugar	Gula
There	Di sana
Restaurant	Warung/Restoran
Eat	Makan
Toilet	Toilet
Coconut	Kelapa
Red	Merah
Later	Nanti
Without	Tanpa
Now	Sekarang
Yesterday	Kemarin
Excuse me	Permisi
Cat	Kucing
Tea	teh
Big	Besar
When	Kapan
Drink	Minum

Remember to congratulate yourself for what you remembered!

Past, present, future

In Indonesian the concept of past, present or future is not given by the verb changing as it is in English, but from using other words that give context to the time frame.

Things in Indonesian either have happened, are happening now, or will happen.

Past - Happened

To indicate something in the past, we use the word **Sudah - Already**. It has already happened.

For example:

>'Have you eaten?' phrase it as 'You already eat?'
>
>**Anda sudah makan?** (Lit: You already eat?)

Helpful Tips: *This phrase is used often in Indonesia as they are very keen on knowing whether you have eaten or not as they like to look after family, and, you are part of theirs!*

Present - Now

To indicate something is happening now we can emphasise by saying it is happening now, although the present is usually implied.

For example:

>'**Are you eating?**' is phrased as '**You eat now**'
>
>**Anda makan sekarang** (Lit: You eat now?)

Indoglyphs™ Language Learning
www.wordglyphs.com

Future – Will happen

To indicate something is going to happen in the future we use the word **Akan** – **Will**. This will happen.

> **'I'm going to eat'** you phrase it as **'I will eat'**
>
> **Saya akan makan** (Lit: I will eat)

Using date and time references

You can use a date or time to relate something in the future or past, like **tomorrow (besok)** or **yesterday (kemarin)**. This again greatly simplifies the structure of the language and reduces the number of words you need to say.

For example:

> **'I'm going to the airport tomorrow'** Saya pergi bandara besok
> (Lit: I go Airport tomorrow)
>
> **'I went to the beach yesterday'** Saya pergi pantai kemarin
> (Lit: I go beach yesterday)

Quiz: Translate these for fun!

- I will go to the beach
- I've been swimming
- I will eat later
- I went to the Airport yesterday
- Saya mau pergi ke Bandara besok
- Anda sudah makan?
- Kamu akan pergi besok?

Helpful Tips   *Answers to quizzes are in the back of the book.*

Indoglyphs™ Language Learning
www.wordglyphs.com

Soak up some more vocab

Wake up thirsty without clothes

Thirsty - Haus
Imagine the roof leaks in your house because it is thirsty.

Hair - Rambut
Imagine you're getting your hair cut near a farm and an angry Ram butt you on your hair.

Come home/ Go home - Pulang
Imagine you are excited to go home to work on your new invention to hang pulleys – called the Pull hang.

Bottle - Botol
Imagine you want a bottle with a bow on it, only you're upset because in this country there's a bow toll!

Knife - Pisau
Imagine someone pokes you with a knife while you're taking a piss – you hear piss – Ow!

Half – Setengah
Imagine you go out to buy half a tea set and you need something to hang it on, so you get the set hanger.

Alone - Sendiri
Imagine when you are alone, you write in your naughty thoughts in your sin diary.

Fork - Garpu
Imagine your new job is to pick up Garfield's poo with a fork!

Indoglyphs™ Language Learning
www.wordglyphs.com

Wake up - Bangun
Imagine you <u>wake up</u> when I hear the <u>bang</u> of a <u>gun</u>.

More - Lebih
Imagine your frustration with the government. The <u>more</u> you try to avoid tax, the more they <u>levy</u> on you.

Skirt - Rok
Imagine you are wearing a <u>skirt</u> from the Flintstones cartoon made of <u>rock</u>.

Clothes - Pakaian
Imagine you are packing a suit case of <u>clothes</u> and you pack your friend Ian by mistake. With your clothes, you <u>Pack a Ian</u>.

Give - Beri
Imagine you have to <u>bury</u> all the presents you want <u>give</u> to your new Dog in the garden, because he hates wrapping paper.

Pen - Pena
Imagine an Italian asking for a pen, he says "I want a pen'a".

Take - Ambil
Imagine that you feel so rich that you can <u>amble</u> over to <u>take</u> your pay check.

Bring - Bawa
Imagine you need training bow to the King so he asks to <u>bring</u> the professional <u>bower</u> to show you how it's done.

Vegetables - Sayur
Imagine you can't say the name of <u>vegetables</u> so you call for the vegetable name <u>say 'er</u>.

They - mereka
Imagine watching your friends in amazement as <u>they</u> play one Spanish <u>maraca</u>.

Indoglyphs™ Language Learning
www.wordglyphs.com

Checking what you've learned

English	Indonesian
Take	Ambil
Clothes	Pakaian
Wake up	Bangun
Bottle	Botol
Knife	Pisau
Vegetables	Sayur
Alone	Sendiri
Pen	Pena
Bring	Bawa
Come home/ Go home	Pulang
Give	Beri
Hair	Rambut
They	Mereka
More	Lebih
Fork	Garpu
Thirsty	Haus
Skirt	Rok
Half	Setangga

Remember you can back over any that haven't quiet stuck!

Indoglyphs™ Language Learning
www.wordglyphs.com

Hot week to move out the village

It's remarkable – even by this stage you have learnt a massive **Eighty Five words!**

After this section we will look at some sentence structure and then review some of the words we've learnt so you can see how easy it is to make your own sentences...

For now, here are a few more words...

Move out - Pindah
Imagine you 'pinned a' note on the door to let people know you will move out!

Still - Masih
Imagine the Superman film is still on at the cinema and you just mus(t) see it

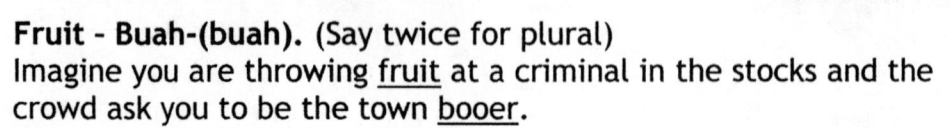

Fruit - Buah-(buah). (Say twice for plural)
Imagine you are throwing fruit at a criminal in the stocks and the crowd ask you to be the town booer.

Then - (ke)mudian.
Imagine telling your friend Ian, if you want to stay happy, then you must get out of that mood Ian.

Village - Desa
Imagine you go to an old creepy village in the hills and it's desolate.

Blue - Biru
Imagine using a magic Biro that writes blue letters in the air.

If - Jika
Imagine hiring a car by letter code and if you had the money, you'd get the G-car.

Indoglyphs™ Language Learning
www.wordglyphs.com

Hot - Panas
Imagine you have got so much food for the barbeque you need a <u>pan as</u> big as the sun to get the food <u>hot</u>.

Shopping - Belanja
Imagine you go <u>shopping</u> for a <u>Bell</u> <u>and</u> <u>Jar</u> for your collection.

Like (Similar) - Sama
Imagine you are building a boat and you pass <u>Sam a</u> hammer which looks <u>like</u> a pick axe.

Market - Pasar
Imagine going to the <u>Market</u> and get great deals and you are desperate to tell a <u>passer</u>-by.

Also - Juga
Imagine Lady Ga Ga has become Jewish, now she will <u>also</u> be known as Lady <u>Jew Ga</u>.

Doctor - Dokter
Imagine a Doctor examining you wearing an Indonesian flag t-shirt!

Week - Minggu
Imagine the terrible <u>week</u> that you got your priceless <u>Ming</u> vase covered in <u>goo</u>.

Many - Banyak
Imagine <u>many</u> Tibetans get together shouting to <u>ban Yaks</u> in their country.

Million - Juta
Imagine a Jew giving you a <u>million</u> dollars, and you thank them appropriately saying, "<u>Jew ta</u>".

Indoglyphs™ Language Learning
www.wordglyphs.com

Young - Muda
Imagine you are an Italian and upset after someone took your young girlfriend. Say in an Italian accent "I'm in a mooda!"

Class - Kelas
Imagine going to an Indonesian language class where everything is painted red and white.

Checking what you're learned

English	Indonesian
Then	(Ke)mudian
Village	Desa
Move out	Pindah
Shopping	Belanja
Blue	Biru
Class	Kelas
Still	Masih
Doctor	Dokter
If	Jika
Week	Minggu
Million	Juta
Hot	Panas
Also	Juga
Like	Sama
Fruit	Buah
Market	Pasar
Many	Banyak
Young	Muda

Remember to congratulate yourself for what you remembered!

Indoglyphs™ Language Learning
www.wordglyphs.com

Some sentence structure

Descriptive word order

Sentence structure is pretty easy in Indonesian, but it is different to English. The main difference is where you put the word to describe something.

For example in English we would say - **"The blue car"**

In Indonesian you say **"Mobile Biru"** - **"Car blue"**

So the descriptive word (adjective) comes after the thing we are talking about (noun).

<Object>   <Adjective>

E.g.

Where is the big house = Di mana rumah besar?

I want to go to the white beach = Saya mau pergi pantai putih

Try these for yourself *(answers on the next page)*

I want red rice...

I want the big brown car....

I want red rice... = Saya mau nasi merah

I want the big brown car.... = Saya mau mobile cokelat besar

Remember, the descriptive words come after the thing you are talking about.

Indoglyphs™ Language Learning
www.wordglyphs.com

Making Plurals

In English we make a plural most commonly by putting an "s" on the end of a word **egg = eggs, book = books**.

Unlike other languages, plurals in Indonesian are very simple. You only need to repeat the noun **(e.g. buku = buku-buku)**, or adding quantitative indicators **(e.g. many, few, number of)** into the sentence.

Most often, Indonesians will imply the plural by the context and not bother to change the word (noun) at all.

For example:

Buku-buku saya = my books

Banyak buku = lots of books *(Lit: Many books)*

Are they your cats? = mereka kucing anda?

Practice using the words you've learned

If you've been following the flow of the book, you'll have over seventy words at your disposal already. It's amazing what you can say with just this many words.

We also know to put the descriptive word, (adjective), after the thing we are talking about, (noun) and how to make plurals.

Use the following to practice your translations. Cover over the English part and translate into Indonesian and then vice-versa.

Phrase	Translation	Literal meaning
I'm thirsty	Saya haus	I thirst
I want some water	Saya mau air	I want water
Where's the toilet?	Di mana toilet?	Where toilet
No sugar please	Tanpa gula tolong	Without sugar please
I want to go to the airport	Saya mau pergi ke bandara	I want go to airport
Where is the market	Di mana pasar	Where market
I don't want this/that	Saya tidak mau ini/itu	I not want this/that
Red rice please	Nasi merah tolong	Rice red please
I'm learning Indonesian	Saya belajar bahasa Indonesia	I learn language Indonesian
It was hot at the beach yesterday	Itu panas di pantai kemarin	That hot at beach yesterday

Indoglyphs™ Language Learning
www.wordglyphs.com

Get some more vocab

Now you're nearly fluent!

Meat - Daging
Imagine you are vegetarian who's cracked and you're gagging for some meat.

Vegetarian - Vegetarian
The word is the same for vegetarian as in English as this concept didn't exist at the time the language was introduced. *You can also say "Tidak daging" (Not meat)*

Isn't it - Kan (*add to the end of a statement to make a question*)
Imagine asking the barmaid in the local, "that's a can your holding, isn't it?"

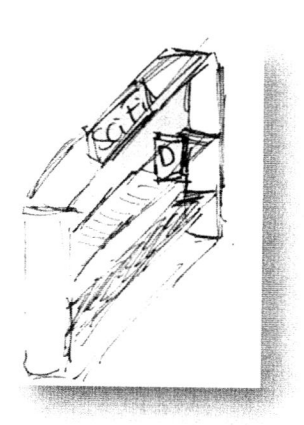

Not - Bukan *(Unlike Tidak, Bukan negates the whole sentence)*
Imagine you're in a library and it's not good because the Star Trek book can not go in the Drama section.

Sit - Duduk
Imagine you have very low ceilings in your dining room. Your friend arrives for dinner and you request they do duck to sit down!

Indoglyphs™ Language Learning
www.wordglyphs.com

Word - Kata
Imagine a guy from Africa agreeing with you about the cat that dug up your flowers – '<u>Word</u>' bro – that '<u>Cat 'a</u>' dam nuisance!

Plate - Piring
Imagine you are on a hard pea diet and drop a pea on your <u>plate</u> and it rings, it makes a <u>pea ring.</u>

Spoon - Sendok
Imagine you are in a fancy restaurant and you've asked for a <u>spoon</u> so many times. Just <u>Send</u> the spoon <u>OK</u> (SendOk)

Glass (of water) - Gelas
Imagine seeing a rather butch girl in a bar with a glass of <u>water</u> and you remark to your friend, that's a <u>gay-lass</u>! (I know it's not politically correct, it's supposed to evoke emotion so you remember it!)

Plastic - Plastik
Imagine a plastic bag with an Indonesian flag on it! (It's the Indonesian word for a plastic bag and a plastic thing!)

Cold (virus) - Pilek
Imagine you get a <u>cold</u> and the pill you need to take is enormous – swallow that <u>pill, heck</u> no.

What - Apa
Imagine you are looking but can't quite make out <u>what</u> is in the rocking chair in your living room – it's your father – <u>Ah Pa</u>!

Bag - Tas
Imagine your latest hand <u>bag</u> is made of gold and looks fan<u>TAS</u>tic!

Light/Lamp - Lampu (Room light)
Imagine being nervous to turn on your side table <u>light</u> because it's covered in poo. You know you have a <u>Lamp – poo</u> problem.

Indoglyphs™ Language Learning
www.wordglyphs.com

Turn (Switch) Off - Mati (lit means dead)
Imagine you turn off a TV in the shape of your friend Marty so much that now it's dead!

Road - Jalan
Imagine see a Jay bird crossing the road calling out its name Alan. "That's a J Alan in the road", you remark.

Stop - Berhenti
Imagine your best friends stop you in a dare as you are about to drink burnt hen tea.

Shower / Bathe - Mandi
Imagine your annoyed you have to take a shower with your friend Mandy as she hogs all the soap.

Checking what you've learned

English	Indonesian
Bag	Tas
Not	Bukan
Isn't it	Kan
Meat	Daging
Plate	Piring
Sit	Duduk
Shower / Bathe	Mandi
Spoon	Sendok
Vegetarian	Vegetarian
Turn (Switch) Off	Mati
Glass (of water)	Gelas
Light	Lampu
What	Apa
Road	Jalan
Plastic	Plastik
Word	Kata
Cold (virus)	Pilek
Stop	Berhenti

Remember you can back over any that haven't quiet stuck!

Indoglyphs™ Language Learning
www.wordglyphs.com

Don't cook ice cream on your Birthday

Photo(graph) - foto
Imagine taking a photo of an Indonesian flag!

Year - Tahun
Imagine every year your love gives you a wonderful silver watch and you say - Ta Hon.

Which - Yang
Imagine helping your spiritual friend trying to decide which they are Yin or Yang.

Very - Sangat
Imagine you are very happy when your friend sang at your birthday party.

Come along (Join) - Ikut
Imagine you are happy when you ask your friend to come along with you to the park and he tells you he could.

Ice Cream - Es krim
Imagine your buy some ice cream and it comes wrapped in an Indonesian flag.

Television - Televisi
Imagine the television is not on. There's nothing on the Televisi(on)

Read - Baca
Imagine going to a wedding as a Bachelor to read your wedding vows.

Birthday - Ulang Tahun
Imagine every year your love brings you Oolong tea for your Birthday and you thank her, oh Oolong - ta hon

Indoglyphs™ Language Learning
www.wordglyphs.com

Help - Tolong-Tolong
Imagine you asked your lazy friend to help, they are so slow the job takes much too long, far too long.

Pineapple - Nanas
Imagine you go to your Nanas and she gives you a lovely big ripe Pineapple.

Teacher - Guru
Imagine you are in India to find out about life and your teacher is a Guru.

From - Dari
Imagine you are coming home from a days work at your organic dairy.

Chair - Kursi
Imagine sitting in a chair at the beach and a big wave gets you wet so you curse the sea.

Cook - Masak
Imagine you are in a "bring your own food" restaurant and ask the waiter, "I've brought my sack, please will you cook it"?

Salad - Salad
Imagine your salad served on an Indonesian flag!

Massage - Pijat
Imagine you go to the animal petting section and are shocked to have to massage a Pigeon at the zoo.

Don't - Jangan
Imagine you feel lucky you don't own a Jag an elephant or a snake.

Checking what you've learned

English	Indonesian
Photo(graph)	Foto
Salad	Salad
Teacher	Guru
Come along (Join)	Ikut
Very	Sangat
Year	Tahun
Ice Cream	Es krim
Which	Yang
Help	Tolong-tolong
Television	Televisi
Massage	Pijat
Read	Baca
Birthday	Ulang Tahun
Cook	Masak
Pineapple	Nanas
Don't	Jangan
From	Dari
Chair	Kursi

Remember to congratulate yourself for what you remembered!

Indoglyphs™ Language Learning
www.wordglyphs.com

Greetings - Times of the Day

Good morning, afternoon, evening & good night

Yes, I'm breaking the rules – but what are rules for??? We're going to learn how to say greetings for times of the day all together!

First, let's introduce **"Selamat"**. This wonderful word has many meanings but is basically used to express **happiness** as in the **good** of **Good Luck** in English. As a result it's used for the good part of **Good Morning, Afternoon** and so on. It's also used in **Happy Birthday - Selamat Ulang Tahun** (Which by the way is literally Happy Repeated Year)

Happiness/Good luck - Selamat
Imagine you want to buy a good mat so you go to a bazar to find a seller of mats – seller mat.

Indonesians break the day up slightly differently than most of the rest of the world. They have four divisions, Morning, Late Morning, Late Afternoon, Evening and Night.

This can be a little confusing to start with, however – most Indonesians I've come across don't know what the time is anyway!

The word **Selamat** is used in front of the following words to make Good morning, Late Morning, Late Afternoon, Evening and Good Night.

Morning - Pagi (Sunrise until 11am)
Imagine you get up in the morning, look in the mirror and your eyes are all baggy.

Late morning - Siang   (11 until 2pm)
Imagine you are going Late morning around 11 to watch a notorious criminal you want to see hang.

Late afternoon - Sore   (2pm until sunset)
Imagine you bump your toe getting up from a chair just after lunch and your friend asks you how it is, you say – it's sore, eh!

Evening and night - Malam   (When it's dark)
Imagine you go out clubbing at night with your sheep who's a great break dancer, you tell everyone who's watching, that's ma' lamb.

You may also hear **Pagi-Pagi** for **Early morning** and can use any of the above with **ini** for **this** morning, evening etc.

Practice these every day and you'll soon find they become second nature. The one's you most often hear are Pagi and Malam, Siang and Sore being less often used.

Checking what you've learned

English	Indonesian
Evening	Malam
Good	Selamat
Night	Malam
Late Morning	Siang
Morning	Pagi
Late Afternoon	Sore
Happiness/Good luck	Selamat

Helpful Tips

You can also say Pagi-Pagi for early morning – the time when you will get the best deals at the market.

Remember you can go back over any that haven't quiet stuck!

Indoglyphs™ Language Learning
www.wordglyphs.com

Phrases & Slang out and about

How's it going and others!

There are quite a few phrases Indonesians use that don't make much sense when literally translated, but are used in everyday conversation and greetings. The most common you will hear is:

"**Mau ke mana**" – literally Want to where!

It's really asking – "**where are you going**" – which, to some Western cultures can appear a bit invasive and elicit a response like – "what business is it of yours?" However, it's more akin to "**How's it going**", the usual response is, "**Jalan-Jalan**" which means "**around**". This saves you feeling like you have to tell the person details about your life, and will, surprisingly, be quite acceptable to them.

Jalan, as you know, means **Road** (or **Route**), Jalan-Jalan means **walk or going around**! So it's like they are asking you "**how's it going**", and you say, "**Oh I'm hanging out**".

You'll also hear "**Dari Mana**" when you arrive from somewhere, like when you come home. This means, literally "**from where**". Again, it can appear invasive to us sensitive types, but it's really just a greeting, they rarely actually want to know.

You can reply "**Baik**" – "**I'm OK**" or as before "**jalan-jalan**" or "**dari jalan-jalan**" – "**from around**".

Indoglyphs™ Language Learning
www.wordglyphs.com

No Problem

You'll also hear this and probably use this often!

"Tidak apa apa" = "No Problem"

You've already met these words, but, because it's colloquial - it doesn't directly translate.

Literally this means **Not what what.** *You might imagine some old British major in the 30's saying this and kind of making sense.*

There's a shortened version of this that you'll hear primarily in Jakarta.

"Gap-apa" = "No Problem"

The **Tidak** becomes **Gap** and the **apa apa** becomes **apa.**

The next section gives you a few more of these colloquial and slang words that are often used in conversations and in text messaging.

Colloquial city and sms

There are many words in Indonesian that are readily spoken but you'll rarely find in language text books or even dictionaries. These have their influence mainly from Java and Bali and often originate from other languages such as Chinese, Portuguese, Dutch and so on.

These words are spread by teen magazines and many radio and television programmes such as (in my opinion) the wonderfully badly acted Soaps (worth watching just for the over acting).

I'm only going to cover the most common here as there are many, however, this will help you understand when the speaker isn't taking into consideration that you are not a native.

The most frequent is the dropping of the initial 'S'. This mainly occurs with the following:-

- Sudah = udah
- Sama = ama
- Saja = aja

Also, in text messages, you may find these words used and or the vowels dropped completely. This make it look like gobbledygook – however you can figure it out – see if you can work this out...

- Km prg k pntai nnti?

Took me a while to unravel some of my friends' texts!

Indoglyphs™ Language Learning
www.wordglyphs.com

There are also quite a few words that are shortenings or modifications of existing words or expressions that stand in their own right.

Here are some slang words you may come across in general conversation and in text messages.

Slang	Description
Banget	This is in common use for **very**. You'll hear it a lot in Jakarta where it's used almost exclusively for the word **Very!** (Derived from Sangat)
Dong	This is used for emphasis at the end of a sentence – just like ringing a bell – <u>DONG</u>!!! If you want to say **Of Course** – it's **Mau Dong!** (Want Sure!) Are you going to Jakarta? = Kamu pergi ke Jakarta? Of course I am! = Ya, Dong!
Gak, Nggak, Ndak	These is a shortenings for **Tidak** – **Not** Often the N of nggak and ndak is so softly spoken as to become superfluous. You'll also find another form of **kagak!**
Kan	We've covered this already in one use, as **isn't it** for emphasis of a statement but I've included it here for more detail. It can also be used to assert an agreement that you already have. **Kan kamu itu rumah** – **yeah, that's the house.**

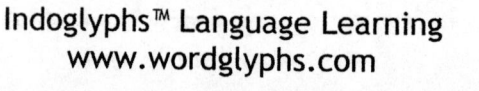

Indoglyphs™ Language Learning
www.wordglyphs.com

Lho	My! You-know! Exclamation of surprise at learning something unexpected.
Kok	An exclamation like saying **"Really!"**
Tuh	This is a shortened form of **itu – that**. It's more or less just dropping the pronunciation of the **i** – like most slang – it's a lazy way of speaking!

That's a taster of some phrases and slang you'll hear out and about to help you navigate the more "street" view of the language. Now let's practice using what we've learned...

Sentence practice part 1

Translate these sentences into Indonesian with the words you have learned so far. It's often much more simple than you expect. Indonesian is a common language for a country with a relatively low level of formal education and has a suitably uncomplicated structure.

Each practice section will help you to cement the words in your memory. Cheat as much as you like, it isn't a test, it's practice!

Translate this	Your Answer
Where is the doctors	
I want a bottle of water	
Yesterday I went for a swim	
I would like some ice cream	
I'd like a young coconut please	
Can I eat this	
What is this called	
I'm staying in the big house	
Who's that?	
When did you wake up	
Good evening, how's it going?	

You'll find typical answers in the back of the book.

Indoglyphs™ Language Learning
www.wordglyphs.com

Some more great words to learn

Late for the dance party

Sun - Matahari
Imagine a hairy man goes out in the sun so it doesn't matter he's hairy.

See / look - Lihat
Imagine you look to see your imaginary friend Lee in an outrageous hat.

Meet - Bertemu
Imagine you meet your friend Bert and he moos at you. Bert, he moos!

Late - Terlambat
Imagine you are late receiving the latest table tennis bat made from fish and sheep, the new Turbot Lamb Bat.

Dance - Menari
Imagine you go to a club to dance and when you look around you notice all the Men are hairy.

Car - Mobil
Imagine your new car has a large air freshener mobile in the window.

Clever - Pandai
Imagine you are in the kitchen cooking a clever Chinese hari kari recipe requiring you to shout pan die at the frying pan.

Find / Look for - Cari
Imagine you are in Rome looking for and want to find a chariot made of solid gold.

Indoglyphs™ Language Learning
www.wordglyphs.com

Party - Pesta
Imagine you make a spaghetti dish for your party and suddenly remember you need Pesto.

All - Semua
Imagine you are on holiday up in the mountains where you can see it all, but, from higher up you can see more.

Driver - Sopir
Imagine you hire a driver and can't see him, your friend says, "So peer through the window to see".

Near - Dekat
Imagine being near someone covered in cats and you're allergic so you have to de-cat them!

Last / Just now - Tadi
Imagine you are happy that it was quite just now that you last saw your Daddy.

Head - Kepala
Imagine you walk into a Cap Parlour and your head is so happy to find such a splendid place!

Bus - Bis
Imagine you get on a bus to go to a show which is so well done up, it's the biz.

Right - Kanan
Imagine you are turning right in a castle blindfold and you walk into a cannon.

Not yet - Belum
Imagine you are disappointed that you have planted some prize roses and you have not yet seen a single bloom.

Every - Setiap
Imagine that every time you are setting up the table, your annoying friend pulls the cloth off.

Checking what you've learned

English	Indonesian
See	Lihat
Bus	Bis
Find (Look for)	Cari
Not yet	Belum
All	Semua
Dance	Menari
Late	Terlambat
Head	Kepala
Right	Kanan
Car	Mobil
Every	Setiap
Near	Dekat
Meet	Bertemu
A while ago	Tadi
Sun	Matahari
Driver	Sopir
Clever	Pandai
Party	Pesta

Remember you can go back over any that haven't quiet stuck!

Indoglyphs™ Language Learning
www.wordglyphs.com

White sand, weather and sauce

Table - Meja
Imagine you invite the major to sit at the head of your dinner table.

Month - Bulan
Imagine your surprise when every month you get sent a bull an' a huge bill for it.

River - Sungai
Imagine you are at a river and you see some guy swimming in it.

Milk - Susu
Imagine when you spill milk on your friend Sue's new suit, they are annoyed, you say "so Sue, sue me".

Turn (Switch) on - Hidup (also means alive and life)
Imagine your computer ran for its life and hid up a tree rather than turn on.

White - Putih
Imagine you must drink a white mug of poo tea. (Yuk)

Sand - Pasir
Imagine being at the beach and asking your friend to pass here that bucket of sand.

People / Person - Orang
Imagine your surprise when you see a person then a group of people with orange skin wandering around your office.

Forest - Hutan
Imagine you are in a forest at night and you hear a hoot and a cry from the tree tops.

Indoglyphs™ Language Learning
www.wordglyphs.com

(Did you figure it out? Orang-utans are literally Forest People!)

Weather - Cuaca
Imagine you are feeling under the <u>weather</u> so you <u>chew a</u> <u>cha</u>rcoal brick.

Sometimes - Kadang-Kadang
Imagine your bike <u>sometimes</u> makes a funny dang noise when you drive. You explain to the mechanic it goes <u>kadang</u> <u>kadang</u>.

Sauce - Saus
Imagine English <u>sauce</u> being poured over your Indonesian flag.

Write - Tulis
Imagine you <u>write</u> a loving letter <u>to Liz</u> – your best friend.

Work – Kerja
Imagine you <u>work</u> in a cottage cheese factory and need to keep the <u>curd</u> in a big <u>jar</u>.

Open - Buka
Imagine you <u>open</u> your web browser to <u>book a</u> new exotic holiday.

Shop - Toko
Imagine going into a <u>shop</u> that only sells things from <u>Tokyo</u>.

Cheap - Murah
Imagine you are so <u>cheap</u> you won't pay for <u>more wrapping</u> for you presents.

Rent - Sewa
Imagine you hand over your <u>rent</u> from your special <u>saver</u> account.

Indoglyphs™ Language Learning
www.wordglyphs.com

Checking what you've learned

English	Indonesian
Shop	Toko
Sauce	Saus
Milk	Susu
Open	Buka
Work	Kerja
Month	Bulan
White	Putih
Write	Tulis
River	Sungai
Sand	Pasir
Turn (Switch) on	Hidup
Cheap	Murah
Sometimes	Kadang-kadang
Rent	Sewa
People	Orang
Table	Meja
Forest	Hutan
Weather	Cuaca

Remember to congratulate yourself for what you remembered!

Indoglyphs™ Language Learning
www.wordglyphs.com

More words for your Indonesian journey

Sorry for the rain and mosquitoes

Sorry - Ma-af
Imagine you are going to hospital and feel <u>sorry</u> to see your <u>Ma</u> <u>after</u> her painful operation.

Mosquito - Nyamuk
Imagine you are exploring a bog and get stung by a <u>mosquito</u> in <u>the muck</u>.

Rain - Hujan
Imagine the <u>rain</u> caused a tidal wave of water while you are on holiday, it's <u>huge and</u> full of rubbish.

ATM - ATM (Pr: Ah Teh Em)
Imagine you go to the <u>Cash machine</u> in Indonesia and it says <u>ATM</u> on the machine - joy!

Peanut - Kacang
Imagine you are at circus and a monkey is throwing <u>peanuts</u> at you which you must <u>catch</u> and <u>hang</u> them on a washing line.

Fan - Kipas
Imagine you are really hot and have a <u>fan</u> blowing smelly air on you because the blades are made of <u>Kippers</u>.

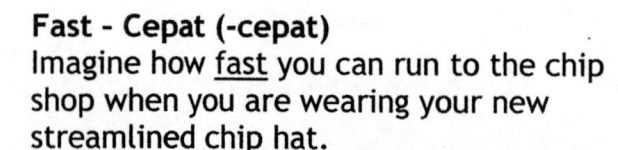

Fast - Cepat (-cepat)
Imagine how <u>fast</u> you can run to the chip shop when you are wearing your new streamlined <u>chip hat</u>.

Flower(s) - Bunga (-bunga)
Imagine your disgust when you give your Mum some <u>flowers</u> and she <u>bung</u> the lot in the dustbin.

Indoglyphs™ Language Learning
www.wordglyphs.com

Everywhere - di mana-mana
Imagine a Manor shaped like a D is here and here and here, everywhere you go there's a D-manor and another D-manor.

After - Setelah
Imagine after eating a big meal your stomach is complaining and you want it to, "settle ya".

Favourite - Favorit
Imagine your favourite ice cream with an Indonesian flag in it.

Often - Sering
Imagine your Dad got knighted and often telephones to brag about it. Sir rings you too often.

Like - Suka
Imagine you really like your crazy cousin even though he's a sucker.

How long (time) - Berapa lama
Imagine someone asking how long the Bear Rappers met the Dali Lama for.

Orange - Jeruk *(Fruit)*
Imagine you are in a hide out bird watching and you see Jay and a Rook mating, so you through oranges at them.

Delicious - Enak
Imagine you are in a restaurant having a delicious meal from a cook who has a knack for cooking amazing meals.

Sick/Pain - Sakit
Imagine you are in hospital sick and in pain after you fell on the Sack Kit you bought to make sacks with.

Try - Coba
Imagine you try to cut your meat for dinner with a new chopper you bought from the butcher.

Indoglyphs™ Language Learning
www.wordglyphs.com

Checking what you've learned

English	Indonesian
Often	Sering
Try	Coba
Like	Suka
Fan	Kipas
Everywhere	Di mana-mana
Orange	Jeruk
Sorry	Ma-af
Sick / Pain	Sakit
How long (time)	Berapa lama
Delicious	Enak
Rain	Hujan
Mosquito	Nyamuk
Fast	Cepat (-cepat)
Peanut	Kacang
After	Setelah
Flower(s)	Bunga-bunga
Atm	ATM
Favourite	Favorit

Remember you can go back over any that haven't quiet stuck!

Yes you can learn many words

Rubbish Taxi's and a place to sleep

Sleep - Tidur
Imagine you have to <u>sleep</u> on <u>the door</u> for your bad back.

Rubbish - Sampah
Imagine your friend Sam dresses up in old rags and you ask your Dad, is that <u>rubbish</u> or is it <u>Sam Pa</u>?

Place - Tempat
Imagine you have a <u>place</u> reserved for your bike and it's broken because someone has <u>tampered</u> with it.

> **Helpful Tips**
>
> *Tempat is used with many other words to signify the place that something happens. Instead of having two words, one for sleep and one for bed, you use **Tempat Tidur**, place of sleep, (also **Tempat Sampah** for place of rubbish - or **Dustbin**!)*

Bed - Tempat tidur
Imagine your room is very small so to sleep on your <u>bed</u> you must <u>tamper</u> with <u>the door</u>.

Dustbin - Tempat sampah
Imagine your <u>Dustbin</u> has been <u>tampered</u> with by <u>Sam's Pa</u>.

Credit for phone - Pulsa
Imagine it scares you how much the <u>Top up</u> <u>credit</u> for you phone costs so you check your <u>pulse</u> again and again.

Taxi - Taksi
Imagine you call a <u>Taxi</u> and a <u>Taksi</u> turns up covered in an Indonesian flag.

Indoglyphs™ Language Learning
www.wordglyphs.com

Money - Uang
Imagine all your money is counterfeit made in your garage so you hang it out of the window to dry.

Ago - Yang lalu
Imagine a long time ago in France your masculine yang friend went to La Louvre.

Originate - Berasal
Imagine your shock while doing family research that you discover you originate from a rare breed of burnt Jack Russel.

Dry - Kering
Imagine you go out for a walk and get soaked through and the only thing that stays dry is your key ring.

Shoes - Sepatu
Imagine your disappointment when you go to the mall to buy some special shoes you can only see and pat and say Oooo to them.

Usual / Ordinary - Biasa
Imagine your friends think your behaviour is quite ordinary when as usual you go to a fancy dress to be as a fairy.

Need - Perlu
Imagine you live in a Palace and so need to buy a toilet made of pearl, a pearl loo.

Yellow - Kuning
Imagine you paint yourself yellow as a cunning way to attract a mate.

Must - Harus
Imagine you are running late and in order to get to get to work on time you must harass the bus driver.

Make/Build - Buat
Imagine you are destitute so <u>make</u> a cake and <u>build</u> a house out of it which is so horrible, people <u>boo at</u> it.

Only - Hanya
Imagine you are a dog and <u>only</u> like to <u>hang ya</u> head out of the car window when it's going fast.

Checking what you've learned

English	Indonesian
Ago	Yang lalu
Bed	Tempat Tidur
Rubbish	Sampah
Originate	Berasal
Only	Hanya
Sleep	Tidur
Dustbin	Tempat Sampah
Taxi	Taxi
Make/Build	Buat
Must	Harus
Yellow	Kuning
Usual	Biasa
Credit for phone	Pulsa
Place	Tempat
Dry	Kering
Shoes	Sepatu
Money	Uang
Need	Perlu

Remember to congratulate yourself for what you remembered!

Indoglyphs™ Language Learning
www.wordglyphs.com

Get ready to start the download

Start - Mulai
Imagine you are on a trip in the country and the weather changes so the cows <u>start</u> to lay down in the fields. A young child remarks, look, <u>Moo Lie!</u>

Besides - Selain
Imagine you go to your local Zoo and they have a special on so that you can sit <u>beside</u> the <u>Sea Lion</u>.

Fire - Api
Imagine you are a pyromaniac and spend ages trying to set <u>fire</u> to <u>a pea</u>.

Plan - Rencana
Imagine you have a <u>plan</u> to work on your car with your friend Ana so you can ask for the <u>wrench Ana</u>.

Help (assist) - Bantuan
Imagine you are oversubscribed by Ann's and need <u>help</u> to <u>ban two Ann</u>'s from your chess club.

Emotion - Emosi
Imagine your deeply felt <u>emotion</u> about your dead gold fish was cut short to just an <u>emoti</u>.

Go out / Exit - Keluar
Imagine you <u>go out</u> to your language class and the teacher tells you to <u>curl your R.</u>

Ready (get ready) - Siap-siap
Imagine you are called to the bottom of the stairs to see your sisters' new clothes and get <u>ready</u> to <u>see up</u>, <u>see up</u>.

Safe - Aman
Imagine you had a bad experience at a pantomime but now you feel <u>safe</u> to see <u>a man</u> in tights again.

Indoglyphs™ Language Learning
www.wordglyphs.com

Olive - Zaitun
Imagine you hear a Greek man sigh as the ton of Olives you are loading onto his boat drops into the sea.

Listen - Dengar
Imagine you listen to the horrible noise your neighbour makes building a den in his garden with a chain saw.

Download - Unduh
Imagine you make a mistake on your computer and download a huge file and cannot undo it.

Religion - Agama
Imagine you are a despot and start a new religion to aggravate mothers called Aga Ma.

Jar - Guci
Imagine you feel exuberant and so buy a designer jar for your biscuits from Guci.

Something - Sesuatu
Imagine you need something from town and your friend says see you at two.

Rarely - Jarang
Imagine you rarely call your African friend and when you do he's so happy he says, "Great man, ja rang!"

About - Tentang
Imagine you are about to come home from a camping trip and remember you can put your wet tent on a tent hanger when you get there.

Different - Berbeda
Imagine you disguise yourself and look so different in your new bird bed, a bird comes and joins you.

Indoglyphs™ Language Learning
www.wordglyphs.com

Checking what you've learned

English	Indonesian
Listen	Dengar
Besides	Selain
Fire	Api
Different	Berbeda
Something	Sesuatu
Start	Mulai
Emotion	Emosi
Go out / Exit	Ke luar
Ready (get ready)	Siap-siap
Help (assist)	Bantuan
About	Tentang
Rarely	Jarang
Religion	Agama
Safe	Aman
Plan	Rencana
Olive	Zaitun
Download	Unduh
Jar	Guci

Remember you can go back over any that haven't quiet stuck!

Indoglyphs™ Language Learning
www.wordglyphs.com

Sentence practice part 2

Translate some more sentences into Indonesian with the words you have learned up to this point. Remember that Indonesian sentence structure is much simpler than English, and you'll probably need less words than you expect!

It's also a good time to go back over your answers to the last sentence practice, and translate them back into English.

Translate this	Your Answer
Stop here please	
I want to rent a room/house	
I don't feel well	
Where is a good place to eat?	
Sorry, I don't understand	
No peanuts please, I'm allergic	
Excuse me, I need a fork	
Where is the market?	
Where can I find an ATM?	
That was delicious	
Is it safe here at night	
How much to go to the Airport	

You'll find typical answers are in the back of the book.

(There's always more than one way to say the same thing.)

Indoglyphs™ Language Learning
www.wordglyphs.com

Unusual Foods and fruits

In Indonesia you will find many foods unusual to you. The most surprising for me were the fruits. I've included a few for you so you know what to expect and can ask for them by name. If you want the best deals, get down to the market at around five thirty in the morning.

Snake Fruit - Salak.

This fruit has a snake like pattern skin – hence the common name. It has a woody texture and a nutty flavour, a little like a chestnut. Makes a nice snack.

Pomelo - Jeruk Bali

Think of an enormous grapefruit that tastes of a mild orange. These fruit are very refreshing and have a thick skin and pith. Peeling one is an art requiring a sharp knife and patience.

Papaya - Papaya (Pepaya)

A Papaya is a large (often longer than your fore arm) orange coloured sweet fruit. It's a favourite for smoothies being easily peeled and liquidised. Contains seeds which are said to have digestive properties (at your own risk!)

Indoglyphs™ Language Learning
www.wordglyphs.com

Sour Sop - Sirsak

This fruit is a spiky (but not sharp) green fruit with a white stringy meat. Has been claimed to have health properties as a cure for cancer. Although this may be an exaggeration by the producers, it does appear to have some properties similar to chemo treatment without the side effects. (Your own research is recommend!)

Jack Fruit - Nangka

Jackfruit is a common fruit for Asia and Australia and considered as one of the largest tree borne fruit in the world. The juicy pulp around the seeds have a taste similar to pineapple, but milder. Apart from canned jackfruit, it is also available as sweet chips. The wood of the tree is used for making various musical instruments, while the fruit is a common ingredient for many Asian dishes.

Mangosteen - Manggis

The mangosteen is an evergreen tree that produces oddly shaped fruits. The fruits are purple outside, creamy inside, described as citrus with a hint of peach. It is rich in antioxidants, some scientists even suggesting it can lower risk against cancer. Don't eat too many at once though, as it can be used to aid constipation!

Rambutan - Rambutan

Coming from an evergreen tree, the Rambutan fruit resembles the Lychee, have a leathery red skin and are covered with spines. Rambutan is a popular garden fruit tree and one of the most famous in Southeast Asia. The fruit is sweet and juicy, being commonly found in jams or available canned. Rambutan literally means "hairy".

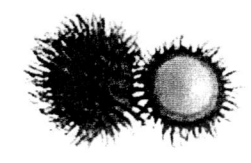

Durian - Durian

Also known as the "King of Fruits," Durian has a very particular odour (it stinks), a unique taste and is covered by a sharp spiky husk. Its smell is often compared to skunk spray or sewage so the fruit is often forbidden in hotels and on public transportation. Still, the whole experience is worth it, considering the absolutely divine taste of the Durian. Tastes a bit like custard!

Noni - Noni

Another smelly fruit – this fruit is another claimed "Super Fruit" high in anti-oxidants. It is most often sold in powder form as a food supplement as the fruit itself does not taste good. The green fruit, leaves, and roots were traditionally used in Polynesian cultures to treat menstrual cramps, bowel irregularities, diabetes, liver diseases, and urinary tract infections. Try it for yourself!

Never, ever, possessions and first.

How to use ever and never.

The word for **Ever** in Indonesian is **Pernah**, however, there is no word for **Never**. Instead you simply negate **Ever** using **Tidak**. **Never**, is **Tidak pernah!**

Ever - Pernah
Imagine your friend asks you if you <u>ever</u> had a perm and you explain, a <u>perm na,</u> no way

For example:

   You ever go to the beach? = Kamu pernah pergi ke pantai?

   No, I never go. = Tidak, saya tidak pernah pergi

See what sentences you can make up using **Pernah** and **Tidak Pernah**.

Indoglyphs™ Language Learning
www.wordglyphs.com

How to indicate possessions & "the" - Nya

You've already come across this in some of the words that you have seen and learned, but not realised that it is actually a modifier, not actually part of the root word. The suffix, -**nya** is used to denote a relationship to the subject or object being mentioned. The relationship is either possession or referring to and object already mentioned.

For example:

    What is that called? = **Apa nama*nya* itu?**

You can think of it as **"of"** or **"the"**.... What is **the** name **of** that?

It's the same when asking the price of something.

    How much is it? = **Berapa harga*nya*?**

Also as **"the"** when referring to the subject of the conversation.

    Do you want to buy the car? = **Kamu mau beli mobilnya?**

And used for possession as **his, hers or theirs**.

    Made went to his house. = **Made pergi ke rumah*nya*.**

    That's her book. = **Itu buku*nya*.**

Helpful Tips: *Have fun with it, it works for any object (noun). It requires good listening skills as it often makes the word sounds like a new word, when in fact it's one you already know with **nya** on the end.*

Indoglyphs™ Language Learning
www.wordglyphs.com

How to say I'm doing that first - Dulu

When someone asks you if you want to do something, and you say, "I want to do this first", in Indonesian we use the term **dulu**.

In this case it is being used like the word **before** or **ago**.

Generally, just think of it as **first** (as in doing that first) and you'll get your meaning across (and understand theirs).

First/Before - Dulu
Imagine <u>first</u>, <u>before</u> you go out your child needs the toilet, they say "I want <u>do loo</u>"!

For example:

    I want to sleep first.   =   Saya mau tidur dulu.

    I want to eat first.   =   Saya mau makan dulu.

    I want to eat before I go.=   Saya mau makan dulu saya pergi.

There are many ways to say the same thing, that's the beauty of language. But remember, to understand what is being said, it's useful to know the various ways words can be used.

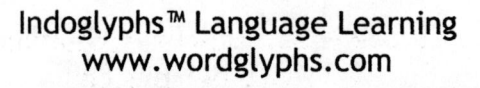

Indoglyphs™ Language Learning
www.wordglyphs.com

You can remember so many more...

Sit down, have a Coffee

Come - Datang
Imagine you <u>come</u> to a rough bar and order a <u>dart an'</u> beer.

Coffee - Kopi
Imagine you buy a <u>Coffee</u> and are so thirsty you <u>copy</u> it on the photocopier.

Until - Sampai
Imagine you are a troll and can't wait <u>until</u> your <u>sand pie</u> order arrives.

Spicy - Pedas
Imagine you go into a shop and ask for a <u>spicy</u> <u>pet arse</u>. (Why wouldn't you!)

This - Ini
Imagine you are in <u>this</u> new band and can't play a song because it's not <u>in E</u>.

Happy - Senang
Imagine you discover a new church with special hooks on the walls and are <u>happy</u> to put your troubles on a <u>sin hanger</u>.

In/At/On - Di
Imagine you are <u>in</u> trouble <u>deep</u> when you forget to leave your tax return <u>on</u> the table <u>at</u> the Tax Office.

Left - Kiri
Imagine to turn <u>left</u> in the video game you are playing there is a <u>key re</u>quired.

Before - Sebelum
Imagine you are training to be a doctor but <u>before</u> you can be a

Indoglyphs™ Language Learning
www.wordglyphs.com

brain surgeon you must remove the "R" from the cerebellum so it's a ceebelum.

Take care - Hati-hati
Imagine you are at a posh horse race and take care not to be embarrassed as your child shouts out Hatty Hatty as the Duchess in a big hat walks past.

Sure – Pasti
Imagine you are sure your stomach cramps are from a bad pasty you ate last night.

Fat - Gemuk
Imagine your disgust as your fat friend eats too much cake, explodes and it gets muck all over the living room.

Brother - Saudara
Imagine you are sad when your little Brother goes to Sudi Arabia on a business trip.

Day - Hari
Imagine one day you wake up and are all hairy.

Broken - Rusak
Imagine your disappointment when you buy a rucksack you buy for an expedition to the North Pole is broken.

Mother - Ibu
Imagine your Mother playing hide and seek with a young baby by saying Eeee – Boo.

On/Above - Atas
Imagine you are feeling precarious flying on a table high above the clouds being held up by an Atlas.

Upstairs - Di atas (Lit: in above)
Imagine you are upstairs and someone has fumigated upstairs with anti Atlas smoke, the place is being de-Atlased.

Indoglyphs™ Language Learning
www.wordglyphs.com

Checking what you've learned

English	Indonesian
Until	Sampai
On/Above	Atas
This	Ini
Happy	Senang
Take care	Hati-hati
Mother	Ibu
Spicy	Pedas
Brother	Saudara
Upstairs	Di atas
Before	Sebelum
Broken	Rusak
Sure	Pasti
Coffee	Kopi
Come	Datang
Day	Hari
In	Di
Left	Kiri
Fat	Gemuk

Remember you can go back over any that haven't quiet stuck!

Indoglyphs™ Language Learning
www.wordglyphs.com

Old pancakes and black phones

Wet - Basah
Imagine going to your school <u>Ba</u>zaar and it rains so hard you get very <u>wet</u>.

Tell me if - Apakah *(Apakah turns a statement into a question)*
Imagine you ask your friend to <u>tell me if</u> a Volvo is a young person's car or <u>a Pa car.</u> *(Pa as in Father)*

Old - Tua
Imagine you are doing some charity work taking to group of <u>old</u> people <u>to a</u> ball.

Difficult - Sulit
Imagine you are feeling how <u>difficult</u> it was for the family when your Aunty <u>Sue lit</u> the house on fire.

Quiet - Sepi
Imagine you get knighted and are <u>quiet</u> when you slip off to the toilet for a <u>Sir-Pee</u>.

Pancake - Panekuk
Imagine you go to a heated competition with a chef making a <u>pancake</u> in a <u>pan cook</u>ing race.

Best - Terbaik
Imagine you go to a bike show and see the <u>best</u> <u>tur</u>bo <u>bike</u> you ever saw!

Dentist - Dokter gigi
Imagine going to the alternative <u>Dentist</u> to have your teeth out and the vibrating <u>doctor</u> gives you the <u>gigg</u>les.

Indoglyphs™ Language Learning
www.wordglyphs.com

Cake - Kue
Imagine you really want to buy cake and a group of Canadians tell you "There's a big queue eh".

Mobile Phone - HP
Imagine you get a huge Mobile phone bill and you are happy to pay.

Expensive - Mahal
Imagine you go for a cruise in your expensive boat to visit the Taj Mahal.

Far - Jauh
Imagine you want to go out to see an old age battle but it's really far to the local castle to see the Knights Joust.

Bank - Bank
Imagine your French friend works in a bank, he calls it a Banque!

Electricity - Listrik
Imagine your friend Liz does a magic trick with electricity, which she describes as a Liz trick.

Friend - Teman
Imagine your cool friend really is the man.

Black - Hitam
Imagine your excitement at your first baseball game when you see a guy in a black jersey hit and run home.

Sweet - Manis
Imagine you are at the circus watch the strong act and you cannot believe how many sweets that man is carrying.

Sister - Saudara
Imagine your joy as your Sister has won a trip to the Saharah.

Checking what you've learned

English	Indonesian
Old	Tua
Pancake	Panekuk
Sister	Saudara
Wet	Basah
Best	Terbaik
Difficult	Sulit
Dentist	Dokter gigi
Cake	Kue
Friend	Teman
Quiet	Sepi
Mobile Phone	HP
Expensive	Mahal
Sweet	Manis
Black	Hitam
Tell me if	Apakah
Bank	Bank
Electricity	Listrik
Far	Jauh

Remember to congratulate yourself for what you remembered!

Indoglyphs™ Language Learning
www.wordglyphs.com

Chat ups, romance and lovers!

Darling, I love your eyes

This section will help you connect more easily with that love you always wanted! Why is this section so late in the book? How could I be so mean? Well, it's to keep you motivated. Of course, some of you, (like I did with my first phrase book) will jump straight to this section. It's a great start – but remember, you might want something more to talk about later! Good luck.

Love – Cinta *(Remember c is pronounced ch)*
Imagine you love having a chin covered in tar.

Darling – Sayang *(like honey or sweetheart)*
Imagine being delighted with your darling sweetheart who agrees with everything you are saying.

Beautiful – Cantik
Imagine how beautiful it is when your football team chants "Ik" for their new player Ickey.

Eyes – Mata
Imagine being happy when your doctor tells you there is nothing the matter with your eyes.

Cool – Keren *(Impressive)*
Imagine being so smooth and cool around your imaginary friend Karen.

Sexy – Seksi
Imagine you look so sexy wrapped in an Indonesian flag.

Hug – Pelukan
Imagine you are feeling amorous and so you go to the zoo and hug a giant pelikan.

Indoglyphs™ Language Learning
www.wordglyphs.com

Girlfriend - Pacar
Imagine your girlfriend fixes clothes and is the best patcher you ever saw.

Clothes - Baju
Imagine you take your clothes for tailoring and a bad Jew does and awful job.

Film - Film
Imagine you go to a film and you see nothing but an Indonesian flag on the screen for an hour!

Dinner - Makan malam
Imagine for dinner you make an excuse for burping while eating at my lamb!

Walk - Jalan-jalan
Imagine you have a long walk ahead of you and it's a challenge, a real challenge.

Holiday - Libur
Imagine you want to go on holiday but have to labour all year to earn enough money. (Remember to roll your R's)

Husband - Suami
Imagine your husband is from India and is a Swami.

Ugly/Bad - Jelek
Imagine you see a bad advert advertising ugly men and the slogan says "d' ya like what you see"

Married - Menikah
Imagine you are at the Church waiting to be married and many cars are in the procession.

Wife - Isteri
Imagine you broke up with your Wife, and tell your friends that your wife is history.

Indoglyphs™ Language Learning
www.wordglyphs.com

Watch - Nonton

Imagine you want so much to <u>watch</u> your favourite show but it's <u>not on</u> TV tonight.

Checking what you've learned

English	Indonesian
Married	Menikah
Wife	Isteri
Darling	Sayang
Sexy	Seksi
Holiday	Libur
Cool	Keren
Beautiful	Cantik
Ugly/Bad	Jelek
Girlfriend	Pacar
Love	Cinta
Walk	Jalan-jalan
Hug	Pelukan
Clothes	Baju
Husband	Suami
Watch	Nonton
Film	Film
Dinner	Malam makan
Eyes	Mata

Remember you can go back over any that haven't quiet stuck!

Sentence practice part 3

Now you can translate these into Indonesian. It's also a good time to go back over your answers to the last sentence practice, and translate them back into English.

Remember to congratulate yourself for what you remembered!

Translate this	Your Answer
Is this the road to Jakarta?	
This is my friend John	
I want a quiet room	
Look into my eyes	
Are you married?	
Is it far to the shops?	
Please massage my feet	
I have two older sisters	
That's cool	
I'm watching a film tonight	
Want to go dancing later?	

Suggested answers in the back as always!

Indoglyphs™ Language Learning
www.wordglyphs.com

Words on the home straight

Is it true your Father smells?

Father - Bapak
Imagine you are not worried that your <u>Father</u> is lost in the shopping mall because he's wearing his <u>backpack</u>.

Fix - Perbaiki
Imagine you <u>fix</u> your speedo on your bike to measure by bike length, or as you like to call it, <u>per biky</u>!

New - Baru
Imagine you are feeling friendly so you let your <u>new</u> neighbour use you wheel <u>barrow</u>.

> **Helpful Tips**
>
> Use Baru with Saja for just now.
>
> Just now -> Baru Saja

Hand(s) - Tangan
Imagine your gang wondering why your <u>hands</u> are so brown and you telling then because you left your <u>hands</u> out in the sun to <u>tan gang</u>.

Towel - Handuk
Imagine you are working at a farm and put your hands in some muck and get a <u>towel</u> to wipe the <u>hand yuk</u> off.

Older sibling - Kakak
Imagine at dinner your <u>older brother or sister</u> (sibling) regresses to a child and screams for their <u>cake-cake</u>.

Indoglyphs™ Language Learning
www.wordglyphs.com

Close(d) - Tutup
Imagine you work for the circus and need to tap a box full of clown masks to close it.

Feet/Legs - Kaki
Imagine you are decorating naked, fell over a tin of paint and now your legs and feet are khaki.

Stomach - Perut
Imagine after your favourite meal your stomach is happy so it purrs and hoots.

Woman - Perempuan
Imagine going to a concert and a woman roadie plugging in a pre-amp who name is Ann.

Jug - Kendi
Imagine your delight to find a jug full of candy in your kitchen cupboard.

School - Sekolah
Imagine going to school and studying so hard you become a scholar.

Police - Polisi
Imagine you have a big mug of Police that you take a drink from and it tastes all Policey.

Straight on - Lurus
Imagine thinking we want to go straight on but are afraid that a ghost wants to lure us round the corner.

Worried - Pusing
Imagine you need great abs but are worried that you are pushing yourself too hard at the gym.

True / Indeed - Benar
Imagine your Gym teacher tells you it's true you indeed need to do yoga to get the beneficial effects.

Indoglyphs™ Language Learning
www.wordglyphs.com

Smell - Bau
Imagine how mad you feel because you have a new craving to smell the bow of trees.

Again - Lagi
Imagine you have rats in the roof so are once again in the loft lagging the rafters after the rats have eaten it all.

Checking what you've learned

English	Indonesian
Smell	Bau
Hands	Tangan
Jug	Kendi
New	Baru
Older sibling	Kakak
Towel	Handuk
Again	Lagi
Police	Polisi
Close(d)	Tutup
Fix	Perbaiki
School	Sekolah
Feet	Kaki
Woman	Perempuan
True / Indeed	Benar
Stomach	Perut
Worried	Pusing
Father	Bapak
Straight on	Lurus

Remember you can go back over any that haven't quiet stuck!

Indoglyphs™ Language Learning
www.wordglyphs.com

Small change for your family under the tree

So / Like that - Begitu (Gitu)
Imagine you know it is <u>so like that</u> Boss to <u>be</u> a <u>git</u> <u>who</u> never gives you time off.

Tree - Pohon
Imagine you are in a fancy dress shop and want <u>put on</u> the <u>tree</u> costume but you're afraid you'll look too wooden!

Younger Brother or Sister - Adik
Imagine your <u>younger Brother or Sister</u> is showing off to your friends and being a bit of <u>a dick</u>.

Man - Laki-laki
Imagine you go to the races and see a <u>man</u> keep winning with the Bookie – he's so <u>lucky-lucky</u>.

Small - Kecil
Imagine you go to a miniature museum see a really <u>small</u> doll of <u>Churchill</u>.

Inside - Dalam (within)
Imagine you are <u>inside</u> a lamp with a genie <u>within</u> <u>the lamp</u> of Ali-Baba.

Loose change - Uang Kecil
Imagine <u>you hang Churchill</u> out the window to shake some <u>loose change</u> from hi pockets.

Letter - Surat
Imagine you receive a <u>letter</u> from your favourite animal Knight - <u>Sir Rat</u>.

Newspaper - Surat kabar (Lit: Letter News)
Imagine you read a heading in the <u>Newspaper</u> about the local tree throwing contest, <u>Sir Rat</u> throws <u>caber</u>.

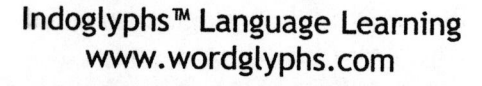

Indoglyphs™ Language Learning
www.wordglyphs.com

Children - Anak-anak
Imagine all your children have a knack of getting themselves into trouble at school.

Change - Ganti
Imagine you saw a huge change in India when Gandi stands against the British.

Family - Keluarga
Imagine your family keeping warm around the new colour Arga cooker.

Under - Bawah
Imagine you duck under the bow of a tree on a walk through the woods.

Rice Field - Sawah
Imagine you are eat rice from the rice field before it is ripe and it tastes sour.

Tall - Tinggi
Imagine you are in India and you go to the famous tall landmark of a tin of Gee.

Turn - Belok
Imagine you are driving to work and need to turn as the road ahead has a block.

Do - Lakukan
Imagine you need to do a paint job but you can't because you lack a can.

Checking what you've learned

English	Indonesian
Rice Field	Sawah
Tree	Pohon
Inside	Dalam
Man	Laki-laki
So / Like that	Begitu (Gitu)
Do	Lakukan
Younger Brother or Sister	Adik
Loose change	Uang Kecil
Tall	Tingi
Letter	Surat
Under	Bawah
Change	Ganti
Small	Kecil
Newspaper	Surat kabar
Children	Anak-anak
Family	Keluarga
Turn	Belok

Remember to congratulate yourself for what you remembered!

Indoglyphs™ Language Learning
www.wordglyphs.com

Numbers & Money

Learning your numbers and all about money.

Indonesian numbers are just something you need to learn to get by. Because there are so many, it's best to learn them by counting and random practice. Once you have the measure of counting, you can try translating numbers randomly until you find you can recall any number at will.

Money in Indonesia tends to be measured in Millions. The exchange rate is very high, about 11,000 to the US Dollar, 18,000 to Sterling and 15,000 to the Euro. This means a grasp of numbers into the Millions is necessary to handle money – that's why I've presented the numbers to that value.

Start by learning the **units 1 to 10** then **11 to 19** and then the **tens**, **hundreds** and **millions**. They follow predictable patterns, so once you have the hang of that, it's quite straight forward!

Indoglyphs™ Language Learning
www.wordglyphs.com

One to Ten (1-10)

One - Satu
Imagine you are in Italy and you see one statue in the square.

Two - Dua
Imagine you like being but your two friends are real doers.

Three - Tiga
Imagine you go to the zoo and see three ferocious tigers in a cage.

Four - Empat
Imagine you are invited on a TV show because you have four sisters who are all empaths.

Five - Lima
Imagine your surprise when you go home and there are five Limas in your living room.

Six - Enam
Imagine you go to the jewellers to have six ornaments enamelled ready for display.

Seven - Tujuh
Imagine seven of your Jewish friends are not too Jewish.

Eight - Delapan
Imagine you want to cook but only have eight dilapidated pans in your kitchen.

Nine - Sembilan
Imagine you go to a look alike show and see nine people have a semblance to the Queen of England.

Ten - Sepuluh
Imagine you go to a club and one of ten knights try's to pick you up, Sir pulls you.

Checking your numbers

Numeral	English	Indonesian
1	One	Satu
2	Two	Dua
3	Three	Tiga
4	Four	Empat
5	Five	Lima
6	Six	Enam
7	Seven	Tujuh
8	Eight	Delapan
9	Nine	Sembilan
10	Ten	Sepuluh

Once you have learnt to say the numbers in sequence from 1 to 10, take a pen and write numbers in a random order and translate them. This way we are able to recall numbers out of order, like we need to in real life.

Also, write the numbers in Indonesian in a random order and come back to the list in an hour or so and translate them back. This will help you translate randomly in both directions. *There's a practice section later if you are feeling lazy!*

Indoglyphs™ Language Learning
www.wordglyphs.com

Eleven to Nineteen (11 - 19)

In the table below you can see the pattern of using **belas** at the end of a base number to get the numbers **12 to 19**.

So, in this case all you need to learn is **"sebelas"** for eleven and you have the rest just from learning **1 to 9**.

Eleven - Sebelas
Imagine <u>eleven</u> knights ringing bells - they are <u>Sir Bellers</u>.

Numeral	English	Indonesian
11	Eleven	Sebelas
12	Twelve	Dua belas
13	Thirteen	Tiga belas
14	Fourteen	Empat belas
15	Fifteen	Lima belas
16	Sixteen	Enam belas
17	Seventeen	Tujuh belas
18	Eighteen	Delapan belas
19	Nineteen	Sembilan belas

Practicing with these numbers as before will help cement the numbers **1 to 9** in your memory as well!

The tens (20, 30, 40....)

The tens from Twenty to Ninety follow a similar pattern. They are simply the units (2,3,4 etc) followed by the word for **Ten** - "**Puluh**".

Numeral	English	Indonesian
20	Twenty	Dua puluh
30	Thirty	Tiga puluh
40	Forty	Empat puluh
50	Fifty	Lima puluh
60	Sixty	Enam puluh
70	Seventy	Tujuh puluh
80	Eighty	Delapan puluh
90	Ninety	Sembilan puluh

You have all the numbers from **One** to **A Hundred** by learning just eleven more words, Yippee!

For the numbers between the Tens, simply say the unit you need. For example.

Twenty three is **Dua puluh tiga**

And so on...

Hundreds, Thousands and Millions

You may have noticed "se" with puluh being used for Ten, this literally means "One" – One ten. The same is true for One Hundred, One Thousand and so on. For Two Hundred, Two Thousand etc. we simply add the units we already know.

Now all we need is three more words to count to Millions.

Hundred - Ratus
Imagine you live in a Rat kingdom and there are one hundred Rat's like us.

Thousand - Ribu
Imagine a Thousand people decide to rib you about your shoes.

Million - Juta
Imagine a Jew giving you a million dollars, and you thank them appropriately saying, "Jew ta".

Here are some examples of larger numbers.

Numeral	English	Indonesian
100	One Hundred	Seratus
2,000	Two Thousand	Dua ribu
40,000	Forty Thousand	Empat puluh ribu
100,000	One Hundred Thousand	Seratus ribu
5,000,000	Five Million	Lima juta
300,000,000	Three Hundred Million	Tiga ratus juta

Checking the base numbers, so you can work out the rest!

Numeral	English	Indonesian
100	Hundred	Ratus
1,000	Thousand	Ribu
1,000,000	Million	Juta

Great - **WELL DONE** - you can now count to a million million - (if you've got the time !).

Ordinals

Ordinals are the words for **First, Second, Third** etc. These again are very simple in Indonesian. Once you know your numbers, you only have to learn one more word to have all the ordinals. That word is the word for **First**.

First - Pertama
Imagine you win <u>first</u> prize in competition to make mothers more attractive and the competition is called <u>Pert a ma</u>!

All the other Ordinals are the number preceded by **Ke**. *Thanks again Indonesia for making the language so straight forward.*

To say **Second** is **Kedua**; **Third** is **Ketiga** and so on...

Now let's check to see how much you've remembered...

Checking all your numbers....

Here's some numbers to translate – see how you get on...

Number	Translate this	Your Answer
24	Twenty four	
19	Nineteen	
5	Five	
132	One hundred and thirty two	
2,000,000	Two Million	
1st	First	
7,000	Seven Thousand	
926	Nine hundred and twenty six	
81	Eighty one	
21st	Twenty first	

Try covering the English over and translating them back.

That's all the numbers and ordinals covered – Hope you got on well. Remember to congratulate yourself for what you remembered to keep up the positive reinforcement.

Date and Time

Months and Days of the week

We are lucky – the months are very similar to months we already know in English. The spelling and pronunciation are slightly different but it's so close you could get away with using the English words. The days of the week are quite different so for simplicity, we'll start with the Month names.

Month names

Month names are very similar to English month names as they are based on the same Roman Julian calendar that we use today. March is the only word that's slightly different – *it's the only one you really need to learn.*

March – Maret
Imagine you are very excited to be getting <u>married</u> in <u>March</u>.

Now let's look at the rest of the months all together...

Month	Bulan
January	Januari
February	Februari
March	Maret
April	April
May	Mei
June	Juni
July	Juli
August	Agustus
September	September
October	Oktober
November	November
December	Desember

Helpful Tips

For June and July, just say the last letter as eee (e and y are often used for this sound in English)

The word for **Month** is **Bulan** (which also means moon) the cycle of which was the original derivation of a month. (The cycle of the moon averages 29.5 days by the way).

Month - Bulan
Imagine each <u>month</u> you go to the market to buy a <u>bull</u> called <u>Ann</u>.

Indoglyphs™ Language Learning
www.wordglyphs.com

What's the date?

The word for date is **Tanggal** – Imagine you are in a <u>tangle</u> from streamers on the <u>date</u> of your 30th year at work!

To say the date, it's the same as in British English but without the ordinal. E.g.

- 4th July – Empat Juli
- 1st March – Satu Maret

It's much simpler than in English where you have to remember the ordinals like 1st 2nd and 3rd.

Days of the week

Now let's learn the days of the week. Really get into the feeling, sense and imagery of doing of these things each week day.

Monday - Senin
Imagine Mondays are days for sinnin(g)

Tuesday - Selasa
Imagine every Tuesday you go for Salsa lessons.

Wednesday - Rabu
Imagine Wednesday is the day to meet the Rabi.

Thursday - Kamis
Imagine Thursday is the day for wearing your camisole. (It's a kind of underwear in case you didn't know)

Friday - Jumat
Imagine Fridays you go jam at the local bar

Saturday - Sabtu
Imagine Saturday is the Sabbath too

Sunday - Hari Minggu (Minggu also means week)
Imagine Sunday is the end of the week and you have a hairy mingy day.

Checking your days of the week

English	Indonesian
Wednesday	Rabu
Sunday	Hari Minggu
Thursday	Kamis
Monday	Senin
Saturday	Sabtu
Tuesday	Selasa
Friday	Jumat

Remember you can go back over any that haven't quiet stuck!

Seasons

The climate in Indonesia is almost entirely tropical with a temperature remaining fairly stable around 28-30 degrees Celcius, dropping slightly in the dry season (especially at night). As a result, there are only really two distinct seasons,

- **Wet** season, from **October to April**
- **Dry** season from **May to September**.

That said, right now its June and it's raining almost every day!!!

The two seasons are the Dry season (Cold) and the Wet season (Hot) and the word for **Season** is **Musim**.

Season - Musim
Imagine you love history and so have bought a <u>season</u> ticket to the local <u>museum</u>.

Cold - Dingin
Imagine you are drinking a <u>cold</u> drink and the ice is <u>dinging</u> against the side of the glass.

Hot - Panas
Imagine you need a <u>pan as</u> big as the sun the food is so <u>hot</u>

To say the season, you put the descriptive word after the word for season. **Wet Season** is **Musim Panas** and **Dry Season** is **Musim Dingin**.

Ah – life is so simple in Indonesia.

Indoglyphs™ Language Learning
www.wordglyphs.com

Telling the time

You're going to need your numbers for this, (at least up to 59), if you want to tell the time accurately. Mostly, I find I arrange things on the hour or half hour to make things easier.

To say the time you put the word for **hour** (**Jam**) after the time.

Hour/Clock/Watch - Jam
Imagine every hour you get your watch covered in Jam.

For example:

- 1 o'clock is **Jam satu**
  5 o'clock is **Jam lima**

Pretty easy – yeah!

So far so good, however, when you want to say the half hour the Indonesians use a different approach to English. They say half to and then the hour. So, 3:30 would be half to 4.

Half is **Setangga** so to say **3:30** is **setangga empat** (lit: half 4)

Otherwise, you can quote the time in digital watch format so 7:50 would be… well, by now I'm sure you can work it out!

It's **Jam tujuh lima puluh** – **Seven fifty** - just in case you skipped the numbers section.

Sentence practise part 4

Now you can use many of the words you have learned to say so much. Have a go at translating these sentences into Indonesian. Also, think about some of the things you might want to say, write them down and translate them. Keeping in mind, there are many ways to say the same thing.

It's also a good time to go back over your answers to the last sentence practice, and translate them back into English. Don't forget; you can always go back over any words that haven't quite stuck to make sure they are in your memory.

Translate this	Your Answer
I just got back from the village	
Really, it was only twenty thousand Rupiah yesterday!	
I would love to meet your family	
I will meet you at 5:30pm	
I'm looking for a house for 4 million a month or less	
Yes, turn left by the big tree	
What are you doing right now?	
I want to move out on January 2nd	
This is my second stay in Bali	

You can check your answers in the back of the book.

Indoglyphs™ Language Learning
www.wordglyphs.com

Congratulations

Well done....

Yes, it's time to celebrate, crack open the bubbly, eat some amazing cake or whatever floats your boat. You have now learned over 360 words of Bahasa Indonesia.

Using this style of learning not only speeds up the process of learning, but it's fun and playful too.

Now you have enough vocabulary to have a really great time anywhere in Indonesia, get a room, bargain at the market, order food, make friends and much more.

This learning style leads you in the direction of the words you are learning very quickly. It doesn't take long before the association you used disappears and the words you need are just there and available for you to speak and write.

The method is very effective and with repetition you will seat the words in your memory for life.

Now, go out there and ...

HAVE FUN with INDOGLYPHS!

Indoglyphs™ Language Learning
www.wordglyphs.com

About the Author

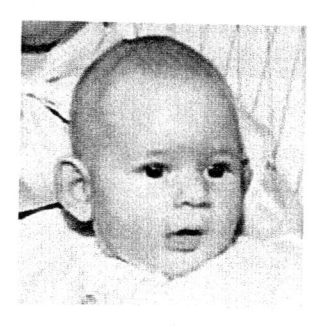

Born in 1963 in Leigh-on-sea, Essex, England, James was always a seeker, loving life and people. James education was marred with difficult teachers and, being shy, found languages a struggle so soon abandoned all hope of ever being able to converse in anything but English.

Educated to Degree level in computer science, James had a thirst to go beyond his seeming limitations. A job in IT Pre-Sales found James needing to quickly pick up communication and presentation skills, redundancy in 1991 gave James the opportunity to travel and expand his horizons.

In 1992 James started to open more and more to connection, he discovered a wonderful dance form called Biodanza and went on to manage a holistic holiday centre in Greece.

Each year that followed led to a richer and richer life experience learning Pilates and the Guitar, becoming a Biodanza Teacher and Improv Comedy teacher.

Since 2009, James has been looking after his parents in England and travelling in Asia, teaching and enjoying the culture and, whenever he can, writing in Bali. James captured, in this book, the method he finally used to overcome his younger learning difficulties. A combination of Comedy Improv skill, an understanding of learning difficulties and a deep desire to share, gave birth to his remarkable book.

Indoglyphs™ Language Learning
www.wordglyphs.com

Personal note from the Author

First and foremost, thanks for buying this book. I hope you find this book as liberating as I have for both learning and for communicating with others in Indonesian. I've made it as playful and uplifting as I can, and sometimes gritty to evoke strong emotions. I am aware it's not the last word on language education, but, my word it's fast and effective.

Speaking other languages requires courage for those of us who have been put down in our communication. The best way I know of overcoming this is to be gentle with yourself, gain confidence from having this memory technique at your disposal and be prepared to be foolish. The majority of people will be grateful that you are doing your best to speak their language and will support you. Those that don't, don't waste your time with them.

Travel is an expanding experience. When you have a local language that experience becomes far richer. When I was in Bali, we stopped to have a coconut from a local farmer, only to discover that someone in a nearby house was having an affair... My trips in the rice fields have never been the same!

Oh – and my love affair is still alive, only, it's a bit one way.

With love, James

Connect with Jai

I really hope you got as much enjoyment out of learning Indonesian as I have. Please send me your comments. Your feedback will help me improve this learning series as it develops. Also, would be great if you could leave some feedback on Amazon. Thanks, Jai

Email
jai@indoglyphs.com

Web Site
www.indoglyphs.com

Twitter
https://twitter.com/EasyIndonesian

Facebook
www.facebook.com/indoglyphs

Look out for the App on Google Play.

- Games to aid Learning
- Phrases by category
- Two way search
- Flick Learning ©

Coming soon...

Indoglyphs™ Language Learning
www.wordglyphs.com

Answers to sections & quizzes

Here are the answers to help you check your translations. There's often more than one way of saying something – you can double check online with many translation services –they are often not perfect – but will give you a pretty good idea. Remember – simple is often more effective than complicated!

Past, Present, Future practice

Translate from	Answer
I will go to the beach	Saya akan pergi ke pantai
I've been swimming	Saya sudah renang
I will eat later	Saya akan makan nanti
I went to the Airport yesterday	Saya pergi bandara kemarin
I want to go to the Airport tomorrow	Saya mau pergi ke Bandara besok
Anda sudah makan ?	You already eaten?
Saya akan pergi besok?	I will go tomorrow

Indoglyphs™ Language Learning
www.wordglyphs.com

Numbers check

Number	Translate this	Your Answer
24	Twenty four	Dua puluh empat
19	Nineteen	Sembilan-belas
5	Five	Lima
132	One hundred and thirty two	Seratus tiga puluh dua
2,000,000	Two Million	Dua Juta
7,000	Seven Thousand	Tujuh ribu
926	Nine hundred and twenty six	Sembilan ratus dua puluh enam
81	Eighty one	delapan puluh satu

Indoglyphs™ Language Learning
www.wordglyphs.com

Sentence practice 1

Translate this	Answer
Where is the doctors	Dimana dokter
I want a bottle of water	Saya mau (se*)botol air
Yesterday I went for a swim	Kemarin saya berenang
I'd like some ice cream	Saya mau es crème
I'd like a young coconut please	Tolong saya mau kelapa muda
Can I eat this	Bisa saya makan ini
What is this called	Apa ini namanya
I'm staying in the big house	Saya tinggal di rumah besar
Who's that?	Siapa Itu
When did you wake up	Kapan kamu bangun
Good evening, how's it going	Selamat malam, mau ke mana

* Remember **se** means **one** of something.

Sentence practice 2

Translate this	Your Answer
Stop here please	Berhenti di sini silahkan
I want to rent a room/house	Saya mau sewa kamar/rumah
I feel ill	Saya sakit
Where is a good place to eat?	Dimana tempat yang baik untuk makan?
Sorry, I don't understand	Ma-af, saya tidak mengerti
No peanuts please, I'm allergic	Tampa kacang tolong, saya alergik
Excuse me, I need a fork	Permisi, saya perlu garpu
Where is the market?	Di mana pasar?
Where can I find an ATM?	Di mana ATM?
That was delicious	Itu enak
Is it safe here at night?	Apakah aman di sini di malam?
How much to go to the Airport?	Berapa harganya untuk pergi ke bandara?

Sentence practice 3

Translate this	Your Answer
Is this the road to Jakarta?	Apakah ini jalan ke Jakarta?
This is my friend John	Ini teman saya John
I want a quiet room	Saya mau rumah sepi
Look into my eyes	Lihat ke mata aku
Are you married?	Apakah kamu sudah menikah?
Is it far to the shops?	Apakah jauh ke toko
Please massage my feet	Pijat kaki saya tolong
I have two older sisters	Saya ada dua kakak perempuan
That's cool	Itu keren
I'm watching a film tonight	Saya nonton film malam ini
Want to go dancing later?	Mau pergi menari nanti?

Indoglyphs™ Language Learning
www.wordglyphs.com

Sentence practice 4

Translate this	Your Answer
I just got back from the village	Saya baru saja kembali dari desa
Really, it was only twenty thousand Rupiah yesterday!	Benar-benar, itu hanya dua puluh ribu Rupiah kemarin!
I would love to meet your family	Saya akan senang untuk bertemu keluarga anda
I will meet you at 5:30pm	Saya akan bertemu kamu jam setengah enam siang ini
I'm looking for a house for 4 million a month or less	Saya cari rumah untuk empat juta per bulan atau lebih murah
Yes, turn left by the big tree	Ya, belok kiri dekat pohon besar
What are you doing right now?	Apa yang Anda lakukan sekarang?
I want to move out on January 2nd	Aku mau pindah Januari dua
This is my second stay in Bali	Ini kedua saya tinggal di Bali

Pronunciation

The following guide will give you a rough idea how to pronounce words from their spelling. Unlike English, Indonesian is relatively consistent in matching sounds to spellings, but there are some exceptions to this, and there are several sounds that can be tricky for English- speakers. The important thing is to give it a go!

Vowels

Vowel and example	Used in Indonesian
a like a in father	datang, nama
e like u in but	selamat, senang
e between the e in let and the a in late	es, sore
i like ee in feet	pagi, siang
o between the aw in saw and the oe in toe	kopi, orang
u like oo in boot	buku, duduk**
ai like ie in tie	baik, sampai***
au like ow in how	mau, saudara****

Note: There is no rule to know which way to pronounce e in a particular word without hearing it first – you can check an online service for the pronunciation (if you're not near an Indonesian).

**the u in the second syllable of duduk sounds more like the oo in book)

***the ai in sampai is often pronounced ay as in day, especially in Java

****the au in saudara is often pronounced oe as in toe)

Indoglyphs™ Language Learning
www.wordglyphs.com

In other cases where two vowels are not separated by a consonant, just put the two vowel sounds together: *siapa* = *si apa*, etc. When a vowel is repeated, put a **glottal stop** (i.e. the catch in your throat when you say "uh-oh!") between the vowels: *maaf* = *ma-af*.

Consonants:

I. Consonants pronounced similar to English:

Consonant	Used in Indonesian
b as in *bed*	bahasa, mobil
d as in *dad*	duduk, saudara
f as in *feel*	foto, ma-af
g as in *good*	guru, pagi Never as in giant
l as in *lap*	lagi, selamat
m as in *man*	malam, selamat
n as in *nap*	Nanti, tahun ALSO SEE ng, ny, below
s as in *see*	siang, kelas Never as in boys
w as in *well*	bawa, sewa Never as in where
y as in *yell*	yang

II. Consonants pronounced differently than in English:

Consonants	Indonesian
j like the *dy* in *Goodyear*	jumpa, saja
k like the *k* in *skate*	kopi, es krim*
p like the *p* in *spot*	pagi, apa*
t like the *t* in *stop*	tas, itu*

*k, p, and t DO NOT have the puff of air they have in such English words as kill, put, and tap.

Indoglyphs™ Language Learning
www.wordglyphs.com

NOTE: When k comes at the end of a word, the sound is cut off sharply (like the glottal stop mentioned above): baik, becak.

| ng like the *ng* in *singer* | mengerti, senang |

NOTE: ng alone does not have the "hard" g, as in finger, which is always written as ngg in Indonesian: tinggal, penggaris

| ny like the *ny* in *canyon* | banyak, nyamuk |

III. *Consonants that need special attention:*

Consonant	Used in Indonesian
c like c in *cello* or the *ch* in *chat*, Never like the *c* in *cat*	cinta, kucing
h as in *house*, but it can also appear at the end of words:	hari, bahasa, sekolah
r like the *tt* in *butter*. It is usually a tap of the tongue behind the teeth, though it sometimes is more of a trill (like the *rr* in Spanish *arriba*, especially at the ends of words	rumah, saudara, kabar

The letters q, v, x, z are very rare in Indonesian, and are mostly found in words borrowed from English, Dutch or Arabic.

q similar to English *k*	Qur'an
v similar to English *v* or *f*	veto, vitri
x like English *x*	xerox
z like English *z* or *j*	zebra

Indoglyphs™ Language Learning
www.wordglyphs.com

Alphabet

Here is how you pronounce the alphabet in Indonesian:

a	b	c	d	e	f	g
ah	bay	chay	day	ay	ef	gay
h	i	j	k	l	m	n
ha	ee	jay	kah	el	em	en
o	p	q	r	s	t	u
oh	pay	key	air	es	tay	oo
v	w	x	y	z		
fay	way	eks	yay	zet		

Index

About - Tentang............ 78
Above - Atas 88
After - Setelah 71
Afternoon (Late) - Sore .. 55
Again - Lagi 100
Ago - Yang lalu 74
Airport - Bandara 27
All - Semua................. 64
Alone - Sindiri 37
Already - Sudah 28
Also - Juga 41
At - Di 87
Atm - ATM.................. 70
Bad - Jelek 94
Bag - Tas.................... 48
Bank - Bank 91
Bathe - Mandi.............. 49
Be my guest - Silahkan ... 27
Beach - Pantai.............. 28
Beautiful - Cantik.......... 93
Bed -Tempat tidur......... 73
Before - Sebelum 87
Beli - Buy 33
Besides - Selain 77
Best - Terbaik 90
Big - Besar.................. 32
Birthday - Ulang Tahun... 51
Black - Hitam 91
Blue - Biru................... 40
Book - Buku 21
Bottle - Botol 37
Bring - Bawa. 38
Broken - Rusak 88
Brother - Saudara......... 88
Brother (Younger) - Adik 102
Brown - Coklat 29
Build - Buat 75
Bus - Bis 64

Cake - Kue 91
Can - Bisa 22
Car - Mobil 63
Cat - Kucing 31
Chair -Kursi................52
Change - Ganti 103
Change (Money) - Uang Kecil 102
Cheap - Murah 68
Children - Anak-anak.... 103
Class - Kelas 42
Clever - Pandai 63
Clock - Jam 120
Close(d) - Tutup 99
Clothes - Baju..............94
Clothes - Pakaian..........38
Coconut - Kelapa..........31
Coffee - Kopi 87
Cold (virus) - Pilek 48
Come - Datang 87
Come along (Join) - Ikut ..51
Come home - Pulang 37
Cook - Masak 52
Cool - Keren................93
Credit for phone - Pulsa ..73
Dance - Menari.............63
Darling - Sayang 93
Date -Tanggal 116
Day - Hari...................88
Delicious - Enak 71
Dentist - Dokter gigi 90
Different - Berbeda........78
Difficult - Sulit 90
Dinner - Makan Malam 94
Do - Lakukan 103
Doctor - Dokter............41
Don't - Jangan 52
Download - Unduh 78

Drink - Minum 32	Friday - Jumat 117
Driver - Sopir 64	Friend - Teman 91
Dry - Kering 74	From - Dari.................. 52
Dustbin - Tempat sampah 73	Fruit - Buah-(buah). 40
Eat - Makan................... 32	Girlfriend - Pacar 94
Eight - Delapan 106	Give - Beri.................... 38
Electricity - Listrik.......... 91	Glass (of water) - gelas ... 48
Eleven - Sebelas........... 108	Go - Pergi..................... 18
Emotion - Emosi 77	Go home - Pulang.......... 37
Evening - Malam............. 55	Go out - Ke luar 77
Ever - Pernah 84	Good luck - Selamat....... 54
Every - Setiap................ 65	Goodbye - Sampai Jumpa 17
Everywhere - di mana-mana 71	Hair - Rambut 37
	Half - Setengah.............. 37
Excuse me - Permisi 32	Hands - Tangan............. 98
Exit - Keluar................... 77	Happiness - Selamat 54
Expensive - Mahal........... 91	Happy - Senang 87
Eyes - Mata 93	Head - Kepala 64
Family - Keluarga 103	Hello/Hi - Halo/Hai 10
Fan - Kipas..................... 70	Help - Tolong-Tolong 52
Far - Jauh...................... 91	Help (assist) - Bantuan ... 77
Fast - Cepat (-cepat) 70	Holiday - Libur 94
Fat - Gemuk................... 88	Hot - Panas.................... 41
Father - Bapak................ 98	Hour - Jam 120
Favourite - Favorit 71	House - Rumah 27
Feet - Kaki..................... 99	How are you - Apa Kabar 17
Film - Film..................... 94	How long - Berapa lama .. 71
Find - Cari 63	How many - Berapa 22
Finished - Selasai 21	How much - Berapa 22
Fire - Api....................... 77	Hug - Pelukan 93
First - Pertama 112	Husband - Suami 94
First/Before - Dulu......... 86	I - Aku 26
Five - Lima 106	Ice Cream - es krim 51
Fix - Perbaiki 98	If - Jika 40
Flower(s) - bunga (-bunga) 70	In - Di 87
	Indeed - Benar 99
Foot - Kaki..................... 99	Inside - Dalam 102
Forest - hutan 67	Isn't it - Kan 47
Fork - Garpu 37	Jar - Guci 78
Four - Empat 106	Jug - Kendi................... 99

Just - Saja 27	Morning (Late) - Siang 55
Just now - Baru Saja 98	Mosquito - Nyamuk 70
Just now - Tadi 64	Mother - Ibu 88
Knife - Pisau 37	Motor Bike - Sepeda motor 32
Know - Tahu 28	Move out - Pindah 40
Lamp - Lampu 48	Must - Harus 74
Language - Bahasa 18	Name - Nama 17
Last - Tadi 64	Near - Dekat 64
Late - Terlambat 63	Need - Perlu 74
Later - Nanti 31	Never - Tidak pernah 84
Learn(ing) - Belajar 27	New - Baru 98
Left - Kiri 87	Newspaper - Surat kabar 102
Legs - Kaki 99	Night - Malam 55
Letter - Surat 102	Nine - Sembilan 106
Light - Lampu 48	No/Not -Tidak 18
Like - Suka 71	Not - bukan 47
Like (Similar) - Sama 41	Not yet - Belum 64
Like that - Begitu 102	Now - Sekarang 33
Listen - Dengar 78	Often - Sering 71
Look - Lihat 63	OK, Fine - Baik 21
Look for - Cari 63	Old - Tua 90
Loose change - Uang Kecil 102	Older sibling - Kakak 98
Love - Cinta 93	Olive - Zaitun 78
Make - Buat 75	On - Atas 88
Man – Laki-laki 102	On - Di 87
Many - Banyak 41	One - Satu 106
Market - Pasar 41	Only - Hanya 75
Married - Menikah 94	Open - Buka 68
Massage - Pijat 52	Ordinary - Biasa 74
Meat - daging 47	Originate - Berasal 74
Meet - Bertemu 63	Out and about - Keluar ... 77
Milk - Susu 67	Pain - Sakit 71
Million - Juta 41	Pancake - Panekuk 90
Mobile Phone - HP 91	Party - Pesta 64
Monday - Senin 117	Peanut - Kacang 70
Money - Uang 74	Pen - Pena 38
Month - Bulan 67	People - Orang 67
More - Lebih 38	Person - Orang 67
Morning - Pagi 54	Photo(graph) - foto 51

Pineapple - Nanas 52
Place - Tempat 73
Plan - Rencana.............. 77
Plastic - Plastik 48
Plate - Piring 48
Please - Tolong 10
Police - Polisi 99
Price - Harga(nya) 18
Problem - Masala 28
Quiet - Sepi 90
Rain - Hujan 70
Rarely - Jarang 78
Read - Baca.................. 51
Red - Merah 32
Religion - Agama 78
Rent - Sewa 68
Restaurant -
  Warung/Restoran ... 31, 34
Rice - Nasi 27
Rice Field - Sawah 103
River - Sungai 67
Road - Jalan 49
Rubbish - Sampah 73
Safe - Aman 77
Salad - Salad................. 52
Sand - Pasir.................. 67
Saturday - Sabtu........... 117
Sauce - Saus 68
School - Sekolah............ 99
Season - Musim 119
See - Lihat 63
Seven - Tujuh 106
Sexy - Seksi.................. 93
Shoes - Sepatu 74
Shop - Toko 68
Shopping - Belanja 41
Shower - Mandi 49
Sick - Sakit................... 71
Sister - Saudara............. 91
Sister (Younger) - Adik.. 102

Sit - duduk 47
Six - Enam 106
Skirt - Rok 38
Sleep - Tidur 73
Small - Kecil 102
Smell - Bau 100
So - Begitu (Gitu) 102
Something - Sesuatu 78
Sometimes - Kadang-Kadang
   68
Sorry - Ma-af 70
Spicy - Pedas 87
Spoon - Sendok 48
Start - Mulai 77
Stay - Tinggal 22
Still - Masih 40
Stomach - Perut............ 99
Stop - berhenti............. 49
Straight on - Lurus 99
Study - Belajar 27
Sugar - Gula................. 31
Sun - Matahari............. 63
Sunday - Hari Minggu 117
Sure - Pasti.................. 88
Sweet - Manis............... 91
Swimming - Renang 28
Table - Meja 67
Take - Ambil. 38
Take care - Hati-hati...... 88
Tall - Tinggi 103
Taxi - Taksi 73
Tea - Teh 32
Teacher - Guru............. 52
Television - Televisi 51
Tell me if - Apakah 90
Ten - Sepuluh 106
Thank you - Terima kasih 21
That - Itu 22
Then - Mudian 40
There - Di sana............. 31

There is/are - Ada 28	Want - Mau 21
They - mereka............... 38	Watch - Jam................ 120
Thirsty - Haus 37	Watch - Nonton.............95
This - Ini 87	Weather - Cuaca 68
Three - Tiga................. 106	Wednesday - Rabu 117
Thursday - Kamis 117	Week - Minggu 41
To - Ke 17	Wet - Basah...................90
Toilet - Toilet 31	What - Apa.....................48
Tomorrow - Besok 28	When - Kapan 32
Towel - Handuk 98	Where - Di Mana............21
Tree - Pohon................ 102	Where to - Ke mana 29
True - Benar 99	Which - Yang 51
Try - Coba 71	White - Putih.................67
Tuesday - Selasa 117	Who - Siapa...................21
Turn - Belok 103	Wife - Isteri...................94
Turn (Switch) Off - Mati .. 49	Will - Akan....................27
Turn (Switch) on - Hidup. 67	Without - Tanpa 33
Two - Dua 106	Woman - Perempuan 99
Ugly- Jelek.................... 94	Word - Kata...................48
Under - Bawah 103	Work - Kerja 68
Understand - mengerti ... 18	Worried - Pusing 99
Until - Sampai 87	Write - Tulis..................68
Upstairs - Di atas........... 88	Year - Tahun 51
Usual - Biasa 74	Yellow - Kuning..............74
Vegetables - Sayur 38	Yes - Ya 10
Very - Sangat 51	Yesterday - Kemarin.......32
Very - Sekali 27	You - Anda/Kamu...........21
Village - Desa 40	You - Kamu 26
Wake up - Bangung 38	Young - Muda 42
Walk - Jalan-jalan 94	

Your Notes.

Notes.

Notes.

Notes.

Notes.